Limit Your Legal Risk:

Issues and Action Plans for the Business Manager

Susan Jarvis

Australia · Brazil · Canada · Mexico · Singapore · Spain · United Kingdom · United States

Limit Your Legal Risk:
Issues and Action Plans for the Business Manager

Susan Jarvis

COPYRIGHT © 2006 by Texere, an imprint of Thomson/South-Western, a part of The Thomson Corporation. Thomson and the Star logo are trademarks used herein under license.

Composed by: Chip Butzko, Encouragement Press, LLC

Printed in the United States of America by RR Donnelley, Crawfordsville

1 2 3 4 5 08 07 06 05
This book is printed on acid-free paper.

ISBN 0-324-22231-9

A CIP Library of Congress Cataloging in Publication Data Requested.

For more information about our products, contact us at:

Thomson Learning
Academic Resource Center
1-800-423-0563

Thomson Higher Education
5191 Natorp Boulevard
Mason, Ohio 45040
USA

To Bruce
  Whose confidence and support
  Made this book possible

And to Ian, Colin, Ted and Miranda
  May they live in a global community
  Where tolerance and civility
  Replace all tensions and conflicts

preface

A major concern facing today's business is the risk of a lawsuit. This book focuses on preventive law by: (i) providing an easy-to-access reference guide to the basic elements required in order to bring a particular type of lawsuit; and (ii) identifying "red flag" situations within the operation of the business which may lead to litigation. In addition, suggestions are offered throughout the book for reducing the risks of lawsuits.

Laws are constantly changing and this book is not intended to offer legal advice for specific legal problems. The reader is advised to seek competent legal counsel when a specific legal problem arises.

table of contents

Topics

introduction

The risk of facing a lawsuit is a major concern for today's business. Potential parties bringing the lawsuit (the plaintiffs) include disgruntled employees, unhappy customers and clients, suppliers, creditors and governmental agencies. Unfortunately, ignorance of the law is usually not a valid defense in a courtroom.

In many instances the risk of litigation can be greatly reduced. This book focuses on reducing the risk in two ways: (1) understanding the basic elements required for bringing a lawsuit; and (2) developing the ability to recognize "red flag" situations within one's business that may lead to a lawsuit. Suggestions for reducing the risk of litigation are offered throughout the book.

Each area of potential liability is categorized as a "Topic" within the book. A "Topic" section explains the elements required for bringing a lawsuit, identifies "red flag" situations and offers suggestions and sources of additional information.

$$Aa$$

Age Discrimination

(For additional information, *see* *Civil Rights Act of 1964*.)

The U. S. Congress passed Title VII of the Civil Rights Act of 1964 to protect employees from job discrimination based on color, race, gender, religion and national origin. To protect employees from discrimination based on age, the *Age Discrimination in Employment Act (ADEA)* became law in 1967. (29 U.S.C. §§ 621-634) The purpose of the ADEA is to protect qualified employees from age discrimination beginning at the age of 40. The law also protects nonmanagerial workers from mandatory retirement based on age. The ADEA applies to those businesses that are engaged in interstate commerce and employ a minimum of twenty workers. The ADEA also applies to employment agencies, labor organizations, and state and local governments. Businesses that are not covered by the federal ADEA are subject to state age discrimination laws.

When the Employer May Be Liable for Age Discrimination: An employer subject to the ADEA may be liable when the employer is found to have discriminated in an employment decision against an applicant or employee who is at least 40 years old and the employer cannot claim one of the three defenses listed below.

Before filing a lawsuit in court, the complaining party must file a complaint with the federal *Equal Employment Opportunity Commission (EEOC)* and obtain a ruling from the EEOC.

Defenses Available to ADEA Claims: An employer charged with age discrimination may claim one of the three defenses available in employment discrimination cases:

1. ***Business Necessity Defense***

   Assume an employer is hiring an accountant and the job requires that the applicant either have completed a course in accounting or have actual accounting experience. A 50-year-old female applicant meets neither requirement and the company hires a 30-year-old female applicant for the position. The older applicant files an ADEA claim. In this case, the employer has a viable defense because the accounting requirement is necessary to the job performance.

2. ***Bona Fide Occupational Qualification Defense (BFOQ)***

   Assume an airline imposes age restrictions on pilots. A 65-year-old male applies for a position and is turned down. A 30-year-old male applicant is hired for the position. The older applicant files an ADEA claim against the airline. The employer can claim a BFOQ based on the Federal Aviation Administration's right to impose age limits on pilots.

3. ***Seniority Defense***

   Assume a 30-year-old female has worked for Acme Company for ten years while a 50-year-old female has been an Acme employee for three years. Both employees work in the same department and apply for a promotion when a vacancy occurs. Based on her seniority with the company, the younger worker gets the promotion. The older employee files an ADEA claim. Acme has a viable defense based on the younger worker's seniority with the company.

Red Flag Situations

1. ***Situation:*** Acme Company runs an ad in the newspaper for a secretarial position. The ad states, "This is a young company with young ideas and young workers." A 50-year-old applicant is turned down for the position.

   Potential Problem: The applicant may file an ADEA claim based on the ad claiming the company has a policy against hiring older employees.

2. ***Situation:*** A local restaurant and sports bar has a policy of hiring only waiters and waitresses under the age of 25. The restaurant claims "customer preference" is a valid basis for age discrimination.

   Potential Problem: The law does not recognize "customer preference" as a valid defense in an ADEA claim. The restaurant may be liable if a qualified applicant is turned down and then files an ADEA claim.

Going Global

As an increasing number of U.S. companies started operations in other countries, the question arose as to whether employees in these foreign operations were protected by the ADEA. In 1984, the U.S. Congress amended the ADEA by providing the law has extraterritorial application with certain limitations.

The ADEA applies abroad when: 1) the complainant is an American citizen; and 2) the company is under the control of an American employer. The ADEA therefore does not apply abroad to non-citizens and does not apply to companies that are not controlled by a U.S. employer.

Defenses Available to ADEA Claims Filed Against Overseas Operations: An employer charged with violation of the ADEA in an overseas operation may claim one of the following defenses:

1. ***Foreign Compulsion Defense***
   This defense is valid when enforcement of a U.S. law violates the host country's laws. For example, a foreign labor law may mandate that all employees retire at the age of 60.

2. ***Bona Fide Occupational Qualification (BFOQ)***
   This defense, available for ADEA complaints filed in the U.S. and explained earlier, is also applicable to complaints filed by a U.S. citizen working abroad for a company under the control of an American employer.

Reducing Your Risks

1. Carefully review job announcements prior to publication to make certain they contain no language that may be construed as discriminatory as to age.

2. Make certain those in managerial positions understand that age discrimination can occur in any phase of employment, including interviewing, hiring, promotion, training opportunities, working assignments and retirement age.

3. Review the latest guidelines on which questions on an application form or during a job interview may trigger an ADEA claim. (Please *see* Sources of Information below).

4. If your U.S. company is in control of operations abroad, make certain the foreign divisions are familiar with ADEA regulations as they apply to U.S. citizens working abroad.

5. Before establishing an operation abroad, seek competent advice regarding the employment laws in the host country.

6. Consider contacting an EEOC Outreach Program Coordinator to speak to those in your company involved in human resource decisions.

Sources of Information

1. The federal Equal Employment Opportunity Commission web site includes information on the ADEA at *http://www.eeoc.gov*.

2. Age discrimination issues relating to employers receiving federal financial assistance are discussed at the U.S. Department of Labor's web site at *http://www.dol.gov*.

3. The Administration on Aging (a division of the U.S. Department of Health and Human Services) provides relevant information at *http://www.aoa.gov*.

4. A discussion on how to recognize age discrimination is available from the American Association of Retired Persons at *http://www.aarp.org/money/careers/jobloss/a2004-04-28-agediscrimination.html*.

5. For additional information, go to *http://fundamentals.westbuslaw.com*. Click on "Court Case Updates" and "Employment Discrimination."

Agency Law

(For additional information, *see Torts*.)

In contrast to statutory law (based on written statutes passed by state and federal law-making bodies), agency law in the U.S. is basically derived from the common law (judicial decisions). Due to the fact that a business is an artificial entity that can only operate through those working on its behalf (agents), agency law is an integral part of the business law environment.

Agency Relationship: An agency relationship exists when one party (the ***agent***) represents another party (the ***principal***) in dealing with third parties. The principal may agree to pay the agent, or the relationship may be gratuitous. In either situation, the agent has the power to bind the principal in certain contracts. In addition, the principal may be liable for the torts committed by the agent in certain situations.

Duties in an Agency Relationship: According to agency law, each party owes certain duties to the other. The duties include the following:

Agent's Duties to Principal: The agency relationship is fiduciary in nature. The agent's duties to the principal include: (1) performing the job for the principal in a reasonable manner; (2) following the principal's reasonable instructions; (3) loyalty; (4) disclosure to the principal of all information relevant to the agency; and (5) accounting for all monies received on behalf of the agency.

The duty of loyalty prohibits the agent from making secret profits or divulging private information about the agency. In addition, the agency must maintain a separate account for agency funds to assure a proper accounting.

Principal's Duties to Agent: The principal's duties to the agent include: (1) payment of compensation (if agreed upon); (2) reimbursement for the agent's expenses incurred in the course of the agency; (3) cooperation in all aspects of the agency business; and (4) providing a safe work environment for the agent.

Types of Agents

1. Agent Who Is Also An Employee

An *employee* is basically someone who works for and under the close supervision of another (the employer). Factors a court will review in determining if an employer-employee relationship exists include degree of supervision; provision of work tools and supplies; method of payment; degree of special skills required; and whether other parties also employ the worker. If an employer-employee relationship exists, the employer may be liable for the torts committed by the employee within the scope of employment. (The employer also has other obligations including payroll tax withholdings and workers compensation.)

2. Agent Who Is An Independent Contractor

An *independent contractor* who also serves as an agent is not under the close supervision of the principal. As a general rule, an independent contractor possesses special skills is employed by other parties, and is paid a commission rather than a salary. In most situations, the principal is not liable for the torts committed by an independent contractor.

Red Flag Situation

Situation: Acme Co. enters into a contract with Outdoor Advertising for the placement of a large billboard in front of the new Acme store. The Acme store manager closely supervises the work, tells the workers for Outdoor exactly where to place the holes and how deep to dig. As a result of the digging, a gas line is struck and an explosion occurs which causes extensive damage to an adjacent building.

Potential Problem: It is possible for an employer-employee relationship to develop even though a contract states the agent is an independent contractor. A court will review the factors discussed above in determining the relationship. If the agent is determined to be an employee, the employer can be liable for the torts committed by the employee "within the scope of employment." This liability is based on the legal theory *respondeat superior*, meaning, "Let the master answer." Due to the close supervision the Acme store manager exerted over the billboard workers, a court may determine an employer-employee relationship existed at the time of the accident and therefore Acme is liable.

When the Principal is Liable for the Agent's Contract: Agency law provides the principal is liable for a contract entered into by an agent provided the agent had authority to contract. The authority an agent possesses may be categorized as *actual authority* or *apparent authority*.

Actual Authority: This type of authority may be either express or implied.

1. Express authority is based on what the principal expressly authorizes the agent to do.

2. Implied authority is based on whatever actions the agent reasonably believes are necessary to carry out the duties expressly authorized by the principal.

Apparent Authority: This type of authority is based on what a third party reasonably believes an agent is authorized to do, despite the fact that the agent lacked both express and implied authority. It is based on what the principal has impliedly "communicated" to the third party by words or actions.

Red Flag Situation

Situation: For 10 years an employee worked for Constructors, Inc. Frequently the employee purchased supplies on credit for his employer at a local lumberyard. The employee is terminated from employment but Constructors does not notify the lumberyard of the termination. Following his termination, the employee goes to the lumberyard, purchases $5,000 in building supplies and leaves town with the purchases. When the lumberyard sends a bill to Constructors, the company refuses to pay, claiming the former employee did not work for Constructors at the time of the purchase.

Potential Problem: Constructors is liable for the bill. When a principal terminates an agent's authority to contract, the principal should provide notification of termination to third parties. Failure to provide notice to third parties may result in a court finding apparent authority still existed in the former agent based on the fact it was reasonable for the third party to believe authority still existed. Actual written notice must be provided to third parties the agent has previously contracted with. Notice to the general public, called constructive notice, is usually made through local newspapers for all other third parties.

In the above situation, it was reasonable for the lumberyard to believe the former employee still possessed authority to contract in Constructors' name.

Types of Principals: Agency law recognizes three types of principals based on whether the third party knows of the existence of the principal and the principal's identity.

1. ***Disclosed Principal***

   A principal is disclosed when the third party with whom the agent is dealing knows of the agency relationship and knows the identity of the principal. Assume an agent with authority to contract signs a document "Adam Jones, Agent for Acme Co." In this situation, the third party knows Jones is an agent and also knows the identity of the principal. When the principal is disclosed and the agent is authorized to enter into the contract, the agent is generally not liable on the contract.

2. ***Partially Disclosed Principal***

   A principal is partially disclosed when the third party with whom the agent is dealing knows of the agency relationship but does not know the principal's identity. Assume an agent with authority to contract signs a document "Adam Jones, Agent." In this case, the third party knows Jones is an agent but does not know the identity of the principal. In this situation, the agent is generally not liable on the contract.

3. ***Undisclosed Principal***

   A principal is undisclosed when the third party with whom the agent is dealing does not know of the agency relationship and therefore does not know of the existence of a principal. For example, assume an authorized agent signs a contract "Adam Jones." In this situation the third party does not know Jones is an agent and does not know the principal's identity. The agent for an undisclosed principal is generally liable on the contract. If the agent had authority to contract, the principal is also liable.

When the Employer Is Liable for the Employee's Torts: According to agency law, the employer is liable for a tort committed by an employee if the tort was committed "within the scope of employment." The principal is also liable for an agent's torts if the principal had the right of control and the tort was "during the scope of employment." This vicarious liability of the employer is based on the legal theory ***respondeat superior***, a Latin term for "let the master respond." The courts have expanded the definition of "scope of employment" in recent years to hold the employer increasingly liable. A tort occurring off the work premises or when an employee is not "on the clock" may still be considered "within the scope of employment."

When a principal hires an independent contractor for an exceptionally hazardous activity such as fumigation, the principal faces strict liability for the torts committed by the independent contractor. This potential liability for the principal is based on public policy.

Red Flag Situations

1. **Situation:** An employee at a checkout counter at Acme has a "short fuse" and slaps a customer who complained about waiting in line too long. The customer sues Acme for the tort of battery.

   Potential Problem: The employer can be liable for the tort if the court determines the tort was committed "within the scope of employment." In this case, the employee was at the checkout counter and engaged in an activity that furthered the employer's interest (checking out customers). The court will determine the tort was within the scope of employment.

2. **Situation:** An employee drinks too much at an office party and negligently hits a pedestrian on the way home. The office party was held after working hours and at a restaurant across town.

   Potential Problem: The employer may be liable for the tort of negligence if the court finds the accident occurred "within the scope of employment." Even though the party was after working hours and not at the office, courts have held such social events are still within the scope of employment because employees feel they are obligated to attend. Based on the potential liability, an increasing number of businesses no longer serve any alcohol at parties hosted by the employer.

Going Global

1. Agency law is different in other parts of the world. In those countries following the civil law system of law (where the laws are codified in writing), agency law is statutory in nature and governed by the appropriate written codal articles. Civil law countries include Mexico, France, and Germany. (The Canadian province of Quebec also follows the civil law system). Countries following the common law system of law (where a major portion of the law is based on judicial decisions) include the U.S., Canada, and England. As mentioned earlier, agency law in the U.S. is primarily based on the common law.

2. A company conducting business abroad may be represented either by a **dependent agent** or by an independent contractor. When a company retains a dependent agent (who functions as an employee) rather than an independent contractor, the employer company may be liable for a tort committed abroad by the dependent agent. For this reason, many companies choose to conduct business abroad through an independent contractor rather than a dependent agent.

3. According to the laws of certain countries, the principal may have to pay the agent

a sum of money upon termination of the agency despite the specific termination provisions in the agency contract.

4. A Directive of the European Union (EU) provides that when an agency relationship continues after the time provided in the agency contract expires, an *"evergreen contract"* exists and, in certain circumstances, a three-month written notice must be provided to the other party before the agency can be terminated.

5. Another EU Directive requires the principal to notify the agent of an "economic conditions alarm" if the sales agent's commission will be significantly lower than normally expected.

Reducing Your Risks

1. Carefully select agents who will be representing the business in transactions with third parties. The business may be liable on a contract even if the agent's action was unauthorized based on the apparent authority existing in the agent.

2. When hiring an independent contractor, do not become involved in close supervision of the assigned work. A court may later find that an employer-employee relationship evolved and the employer is liable for the torts of the former independent contractor (who is now considered an employee).

3. Make certain that proper notification is given to third parties when terminating a former employee's authority to contract in the company's name; otherwise, the company may be liable on a contract entered into by an employee who was discharged from employment.

4. When hiring employees keep in mind the employer's potential liability if the employee commits a tort "within the scope of employment." For example, don't hire a reckless driver to make deliveries for the company.

5. Consider retaining independent contractors rather than dependent agents to conduct business for the company abroad; otherwise, the principal/employer may be liable for torts committed by the agent/employee "within the scope of employment."

6. Seek competent advice prior to entering into any agency relationship abroad in order to understand and assess the potential liability for any actions taken by the agent in the foreign country.

7. Seek advice on agency laws in the host country that may impact the agreement your company has with an overseas dependent agent or independent contractor.

Sources of Information

1. Additional information on agency law is available at *http://www.law.cornell.edu/topics/agency.html.*

2. For information on the European Union Directives, visit *http://europa.eu.int/eur-lex/en/.* Click on "The European Union Online."

3. For additional information, go to *http://fundamentals.westbuslaw.com.* Click on "Court Case Updates" and then "Agency."

Alien Tort Claims Act

(For additional information, *see Torts*.)

In 1789, the U. S. Congress passed the ***Alien Tort Claims Act (ATCA)*** (28 U.S.C. § 1350) as part of the federal Judiciary Act. The ATCA provides "...the district Courts shall have original jurisdiction of any civil action by an alien for a tort only, committed in violation of the law of nations or a treaty of the United States." Infrequently used for nearly 200 years, the ATCA has recently become the basis of lawsuits against U.S. private companies' overseas operations. Plaintiff complaints include allegations that failure to obtain adequate informed consent prior to conducting medical tests violates international law. Tort liability is also sought by alien plaintiffs claiming harm by foreign law enforcement agents and foreign governments.

Going Global

An increasing number of U.S. companies with overseas operations are being sued by alien workers for alleged torts that occurred at the overseas sites. These cases, based on the ACTA, are brought in federal district courts in the U.S.

Reducing Your Risks

1. Understand that the Alien Tort Claims Act allows alien workers in your U.S.-based overseas operations to bring a lawsuit in U.S. District Court if the alleged tort violates international law or a treaty.

2. Recognize that recent lawsuits under the ATCA have alleged tort liability on the defendant company's part for the alleged atrocities committed by representatives of foreign governments, including military personnel.

3. Monitor the latest court decisions relevant to lawsuits brought against U.S. companies under the ATCA.

Sources of Information

1. To learn more about the ATCA, *see* 116 Harvard Law Review 1525 (March, 2003).

2. Additional information is found at 42 Columbia Journal of Transnational Law 153 (2003).

Alternative Dispute Resolution

An increasing number of domestic and international contracts include clauses providing that if a dispute arises, the parties agree to resolve the dispute through a means other than litigation. This alternative to courtroom litigation is referred to as *Alternative Dispute Resolution (ADR)*. When the parties did not agree in advance to ADR and a lawsuit is filed, both state and federal courts encourage ADR as an alternative to litigation. As a result of this policy, a high percentage of claims filed in the courts are now settled through ADR before litigation begins.

Advantages of ADR

1. Settling a dispute by ADR may be cheaper monetarily than litigation.

2. A settlement is reached in a shorter period of time and the injured party is compensated in a timely manner.

3. The third party utilized in mediation or arbitration is usually knowledgeable in the area of business the dispute involves and therefore brings an expertise to the process that is ordinarily not available in the litigation process.

4. By utilizing ADR, the parties avoid the adverse publicity frequently associated with a high-profile lawsuit.

5. A lawsuit can tie up key company managers and employees for an extensive period of time and thereby hurt company productivity. The use of ADR reduces this loss.

6. Litigation takes an emotional toll on both parties to the lawsuit. The use of ADR usually is less traumatic for all concerned.

Disadvantages of ADR

1. When the dispute is settled through arbitration, the losing party generally cannot take the matter to court.

2. Settlements reached through ADR do not establish a "precedent" applicable to later similar disputes.

3. By utilizing ADR, the parties may not have the means of discovering as much evi-

dence as they could through the rules of evidence available in litigation.

Means of ADR: The three most commonly used means of ADR include negotiation, mediation and arbitration:

1. *Negotiation*

In this process, the parties attempt to settle the dispute between themselves. Frequently each party will have an attorney present during the negotiation process but the parties function as their own negotiators.

2. *Mediation*

A third party mediator listens to both sides of the dispute and attempts to bring the parties to agreement. The mediator does not issue a decision and if either party is dissatisfied, that party may resort to litigation.

3. *Arbitration*

A third party arbitrator (or panel of arbitrators) listens to both sides and then renders a decision. As a general rule, the arbitrator's decision is binding. If the losing party then attempts to sue in court, the judge will generally uphold the arbitrator's decision and refuse to hear the case in court. The court may not enforce the arbitrator's decision when there were improprieties or illegalities in the arbitration process. For example, the arbitration decision would not be enforced if the winning party bribed the arbitrator or the losing party was mentally incompetent when entering into the original contract.

Occasionally the parties to a dispute will agree to nonbinding arbitration. In this situation, the party losing in arbitration can then file a lawsuit. If a judge refers a lawsuit to arbitration, the party losing in arbitration can also continue with the lawsuit.

A number of organizations provide professional arbitrators to hear disputes. These include the American Arbitration Association and the International Chamber of Commerce.

Red Flag Situation

Situation: The owner of a Denver florist enters into a contract to purchase 500 dozen red roses for Valentine's Day to be delivered on February 10. The roses arrive two days late and the florist wants to sue for the profits lost due to the late delivery. The attorney for the injured party points out the contract provides for arbitration in case of a dispute. The owner of the florist claims she did not have time to read the entire contract or she would never have agreed to arbitration.

Potential Problem: Frequently a party will sign a contract without carefully reading all of the fine print. The contract may contain an arbitration clause providing the party gives up all rights to bring a lawsuit in case of a dispute. Failure to carefully read a contract may result in later "surprises" that the party would never have agreed to. This failure to read the contract is not a valid excuse. In the above example, the florist must submit the dispute to arbitration.

In certain situations involving a contract for goods between two merchants, the acceptance may include additional terms that were not included in the offer. These additional terms may include an arbitration provision. In certain circumstances the court may enforce the arbitration provision if the party making the offer does not object in a timely manner. (See Sales Contracts for a further discussion of contracts for the sale of goods.)

Going Global

1. An increasing number of international contracts provide for ADR in case a dispute arises. When the contract provides for arbitration, the winning party may have a problem enforcing the arbitration award in the foreign party's country. Several international treaties address this problem. Over 100 countries have signed the U.N. Convention on the Recognition and Enforcement of Foreign Arbitral Awards (the New York Convention) whereby the signatory countries agree to enforce these arbitration awards.

2. A number of organizations provide arbitration services for international contracts. These include the International Chamber of Commerce and the U.N. Commission for International Trade Law.

3. A problem that frequently arises in international contracts involves the interpretation of a particular word or business term. The contracting parties may include a choice of language provision in the contract providing that in case of a dispute over the definition of a word or business term, which language will prevail. This choice of language provision can be included in a contract that also provides for ADR.

Reducing Your Risks

1. When entering into a domestic or international contract, consider the advantages (and disadvantages) of including an ADR clause in the contract.

2. In certain situations, the courts have not enforced an arbitration clause in a consumer contract based on the fact the court considered the contract or the clause to be unconscionable (taking unfair advantage of the consumer). (For additional information, *see Contracts.*) If your company includes an arbitration clause in a consumer contract, have the contract reviewed to make certain the arbitration clause will be enforceable.

3. Be familiar with the various organizations offering arbitration services and the arbitration rules the organization follows.

4. Seek competent advice prior to entering into any international contract providing for arbitration to make certain all aspects of the contract are enforceable under the laws of the other party's country.

5. Read all contracts carefully before signing; ignorance of contractual terms is no defense for noncompliance. In certain situations, you may not want to relinquish the right to sue.

Sources of Information

1. Information on mediation and arbitration services is available through the Center for Public Resource Institution for Dispute Resolution at *http://www.cpradr.org.*

2. The International Chamber of Commerce provides information on its ADR services at *http://www.iccwbo.org.index_courts.asp.* Click on "ICC International Court of Arbitration."

3. The World Bank provides ADR information at *http://www.worldbank.org.* Go to "Search" and type in "Alternative Dispute Resolution."

4. Additional ADR information is available through *http://www.law.cornell.edu.*

5. For more information, go to *http://www.swlearning.com/blaw/fundamentals/ fundamentals5e/fundamentals5e.html.* Click on "Court Case Updates" and then "Alternate Dispute Resolution."

Americans With Disabilities Act

In 1990, the federal *Americans With Disabilities Act (ADA)* was implemented to protect the disabled. The law prohibits an employer from discriminating against an otherwise qualified applicant or employee if the individual can perform the required work provided the employer makes a *"reasonable accommodation"* for the disability. In addition, the ADA prohibits discrimination in public accommodations, commercial facilities, and state and local governments. Before filing a lawsuit in court, the complainant must first file a complaint and seek a ruling from the Equal Employment Opportunity Commission (EEOC).

Requirements for Prevailing in an ADA Claim: The law specifies what is required in ordered for a disabled person to win an ADA claim based on employment discrimination and commercial facilities.

In order to prevail in an employment suit, the claimant must prove that he or she:

(1) has a mental or physical impairment that has been designated as a disability; (2) is qualified to perform the work; and (3) the employer discriminated against the claimant based exclusively on the disability. The employer is not liable if the claimant is unable to prove all three of the above elements.

Impairments Designated As Disabilities: According to the law, a disabled person is one who: (1) has a mental or physical impairment substantially limiting one or more major life activities; (2) has a record of such impairment; or (3) is regarded as having such an impairment.

Among the impairments considered as disabilities are alcoholism, cancer, blindness, paraplegia, diabetes, acquired immune deficiency syndrome (AIDS) and obesity wherein the claimant's weight exceeds the normal weight by at least two times ("morbid obesity"). Other impairments include heart disease, cerebral palsy, and muscular dystrophy. The U.S. Supreme Court has ruled that a person with an HIV infection is disabled even though the person has not manifested any symptoms of AIDS.

Red Flag Situation

Situation: A female applicant applies for a job with Acme Co. She was diagnosed with cancer ten years ago but is now considered cured. Concerned that her cancer may recur and raise the company's insurance premiums, Acme refuses to hire the qualified applicant.

Potential Problem: An ADA claimant does not have to be currently suffering from a disability in order to file a claim. The claimant is also considered disabled when the claimant has a past history of suffering from one of the designated impairments or is regarded by others as having the impairment. In this situation, the qualified applicant may successfully file an ADA claim.

Duty to Provide Reasonable Accommodations: The ADA requires an employer to provide reasonable accommodations to an otherwise qualified applicant or employee provided the accommodations do not impose an undue hardship on the employer.

Red Flag Situation

Situation: An applicant for a secretarial position at Acme Co. is hearing impaired. The otherwise qualified applicant is denied the position based on the impairment. The impairment can be accommodated by Acme purchasing an inexpensive hearing amplifier to place on the telephone the applicant would use in the office.

Potential Problem: Acme may be liable for refusing to make a reasonable accommodation for the applicant's disability. An employer may refuse to provide an accommodation for a disabled employee when the accommodation results in an undue hardship for the employer. In this example, the inexpensive amplifier would not be considered an undue hardship.

The courts will determine on a case-by-case basis what constitutes an undue hardship on the employer.

Going Global

The ADA applies abroad when the complainant is an American citizen and the company is under the control of an American employer. Defenses available in claims filed abroad include:

1. *Foreign Compulsion Defense*

This defense is valid when enforcement of a U.S. law violates the host country's laws.

2. *Bona Fide Occupation Qualification (BFOQ)*

Assume a female U.S. citizen who is morbidly obese applies for a job as a model for a woman's clothing shop in Paris. The shop is under the control of a U.S. department store chain and sells only petite sized clothes. None of the clothes fit the applicant and she is turned down for the job. She then files an ADA complaint and claims discrimination based on her obesity. The employer can claim the BFOQ defense because the job required a petite-sized model.

Reducing Your Risks

1. Carefully review job announcements prior to publication for any language that may be considered discriminatory as to disabilities.

2. Review the latest EEOC regulations regarding what is considered an impairment on a regular basis.

3. Seek competent counsel regularly regarding what questions (if any) relative to impairments are illegal on job application forms and during the interview process. Rules regarding these questions are changing and what may be appropriate one week may be considered discriminatory a short time later.

4. Review your state's laws relevant to discrimination against the disabled.

5. If your company is in control of foreign operations, confirm the foreign divisions are familiar with the latest ADA regulations as they apply to U.S. citizens working abroad.

6. Understand that the ADA also requires adequate accommodations such as parking places and rest room facilities for members of the public who are disabled and

who will be coming to your place of business. Make certain that you are meeting these requirements.

Sources of Information

1. The federal Equal Employment Opportunity Commission provides ADA information at *http://www.eeoc.gov.*

2. Information on ADA is provided by the federal Department of Justice at *http://www.usdoj.gov/crt/ada/adahom1.htm.*

3. A summary of the ADA is provided by the federal Department of Labor at *http://www.dol.gov/odep/pubs/misc/summada.htm.*

4. For more information and frequently asked questions, visit *http://www.dol.gov/odep/faqs/main.htm.*

5. Additional information is available at *http://fundamentals.westbuslaw.com.* Click on "Court Case Updates" and "Employment Discrimination."

Arbitration

(For additional information, *see **Alternative Dispute Resolution**.*)

A major means of ***Alternative Dispute Resolution (ADR)***. A third party neutral ***arbitrator*** (or a panel of arbitrators) listens to all sides and renders a decision. As a general rule, the arbitrator's decision is binding. If the losing party then attempts to sue in court, the judge will uphold the arbitrator's decision and refuse to hear the case in court. The court may not enforce the arbitrator's decision when there were improprieties or illegalities in the arbitration process. For example, the arbitration decision would not be enforced if the winning party bribed the arbitrator(s) or the losing party was mentally incompetent when entering into the original contract.

Artisan's Lien

(For additional information, *see **Secured Transactions**.*)

A major concern of a business is how to assure payment for goods or services it provides to another party. One way a creditor can protect its interest is through a lien. An ***artisan's lien*** is a security device for a party providing materials or services (labor) for the repair of tangible personal (movable) property. The creditor may retain this possessory lien on the property until the property owner pays for the materials or services provided. As a general rule, the lien applies when the property owner agreed to pay cash upon completion of the job and the lien holder maintains possession of the property. In most states, the lien holder can foreclose on the lien and sell the property after meeting specific statutory requirements. The lien holder must provide notice to the debtor before the sale in accordance with state law. Procedures for foreclosure sales may vary from one state to another.

In many states, an artisan lien may also apply when services are provided for the care of animals, such as the veterinarian's care of a horse.

Red Flag Situation

> ***Situation:*** A tire store replaces all four tires on a customer's sports car. The customer had agreed to pay upon completion of the job but refuses. A technician for the tire store releases the car when the customer promises to return "soon" with the promised payment.
>
> ***Potential Problem:*** When a party holding an artisan's lien on personal property relinquishes the property, the lien is extinguished. In this situation, release of the sports car also releases the possessory artisan's lien and the tire store must seek other recourse to assure payment.

Going Global

The laws on liens vary from one country to another. If your company provides materials or services for the repair on personal property abroad, the requirements for holding a lien on the property in the case of nonpayment may be quite different from U.S. law. In Canada, the possessory lien described in this section is referred to as the "repairer's lien" and applies when services are provided to improve, restore or maintain the goods.

Reducing Your Risks

1. Inform your employees that release of a repaired item prior to payment results in the loss of the possessory artisan's lien.

2. Seek legal advice prior to exercising your artisan's lien. Failure to comply with

state laws relevant to notice to debtor, conducting the foreclosure sale, and payment of excess sales proceeds to the debtor may result in legal liability to the debtor.

3. If your company provides materials or services for repairing personal property in overseas operations, become familiar with the host country's requirements for obtaining a valid lien on the property in case of nonpayment.

Sources of Information

1. Cornell University's Legal Information Institute provides additional information on liens at *http://www.law.cornell.edu/topics/debtor_creditor.html*.

2. To learn more, go to *http://fundamentals.westbuslaw.com*. Click on "Interactive Study Guide." Scroll to chapter 21, "Creditor's Rights and Bankruptcy."

Assault

(For additional information, *see Torts*.)

Many lawsuits brought against businesses today are based on the commission of a tort. Tort law involves a private wrong (rather than a criminal act) and their own private attorneys represent the parties. Torts fall into three categories: intentional torts, negligence, and strict liability.

The intentional tort of ***assault*** occurs when the defendant intentionally engages in an act that threatens the plaintiff, the injured party. (The tort of assault is different from the criminal activity defined as assault.)

Elements of Assault: For the plaintiff to prevail in the tort action, the plaintiff must prove four elements:

1. the defendant intended the act which threatens or places the plaintiff in fear;

2. the harm the plaintiff perceives is imminent harm;

3. the apprehension is experienced by the plaintiff; and

4. it is reasonable for the plaintiff to experience such apprehension.

Assume a salesperson for Acme Company loses patience with a customer, picks up a sales manual and throws it at the customer. The customer sees the book flying toward her and experiences apprehension. An assault has occurred.

When the Employer May Be Liable: According to agency law, the employer may be liable for a tort committed by an employee "within the scope of employment." In the above example, Acme Company faces liability for the employee's assault, which was committed "within the scope of employment." If, however, the manual was thrown as a result of a long-standing feud between the two parties and had nothing to do with the employee's work assignment, the employer would not be liable.

Defense Available in an Assault Claim: A party charged with the tort of assault may claim consent if the plaintiff consented to the defendant's action. Assume a professional boxer goes into the boxing ring. The opponent raises a glove, swings and hits the first boxer who saw the painful blow coming. By entering into the ring, the boxer assumed the risk of suffering the tort of assault.

Red Flag Situation

Situation: A careless employee in a sporting goods store tosses a ball at an elderly customer as a joke. The customer sees the ball approaching becomes apprehensive and suffers a panic attack.

Potential Problem: The employee may be liable for assault even if the ball never hit the victim. The tort of assault does not require that the defendant intended actual harm to the victim; a prank that meets the four elements of assault can result in liability. The sporting goods store also faces potential liability based on agency law.

Going Global

Tort laws vary from one country to another. In those countries that follow the civil law system of law, tort law is found in the written civil codal articles. In common law countries, tort law is generally based on prior judicial decisions. One of the risks of conducting business abroad through dependent agents (employees) is the potential liability of the employer for the torts committed by the employee. (*see Agency Law.*)

Reducing Your Risks

1. Advise your employees of the risks associated with throwing items, even as a joke, toward other employees and customers. Emphasize that the tort of assault does not require actual intent to harm on the defendant's part.

2. Make certain employees understand that the employer faces potential tort liability for any tort the employee commits "within the scope of employment."

3. If your company has overseas operations, become familiar with tort laws in the host country. These laws may vary significantly from U.S. tort laws.

Sources of Information

1. Additional information on tort law is available through the Internet Law Library at *http://www.lawguru.com/ilawlib.*

2. To learn more about torts, go to *http://www.swlearning.com/blaw/ fundamentals/fundamentals5e/fundamentals5e.html.* Go to "Internet Applications" and click on Chapter 5, "Torts."

Assignment of Rights

(For additional information, *see Contracts.*)

A major source of business disputes today involves contracts. Frequently one of the parties to the original contract participates in an ***assignment of rights*** to a third party. In this situation, the ***assignee*** (the party to whom the rights are assigned) assumes the rights the ***assignor*** (the party making the assignment) had against the other party to the original contract. Assume buyer agrees to pay seller $500 in thirty days in exchange for seller's used car. Seller (assignor) can assign his right to collect the $500 to an assignee. The assignee has the right to sue buyer if the latter refuses to pay the $500.

Certain rights, including the right to an individual's personal service, cannot be assigned. Assume a singer has agreed to perform at a club. The club owner cannot assign the right to the personal performance. Statutory law may also prohibit the assignment of contractual rights. For example, the recipient of worker's compensation cannot assign the right to collect monthly payments to another party.

Red Flag Situation

Situation: A customer buys a car on credit from an auto dealer. The auto dealer "sells" the right to collect the $23,000 over 36 months to a finance company for $20,000 cash. The finance company fails to notify customer of the assignment and the customer makes her next monthly payment to the auto dealer. The dealer leaves town with the money and the customer refuses to make the payment to the finance company.

Potential Problem: When the assignee fails to notify the debtor of the assignment and the debtor continues to pay the assignor, the assignee has no cause of action against the debtor for the payment made to the assignor. The assignee's only recourse is against the assignor. It is therefore important that the assignee immediately notify the original debtor in writing of the assignment.

Going Global

Contract law varies from one country to another. If your company is the assignee of the contractual right to collect money arising from a contract in another country, make certain the right is legally assignable and that you are in compliance with the notification requirements of that country.

Reducing Your Risks

1. A creditor may "sell" at discount the right to collect a debt in the future. This assignment of a right to collect a future debt occurs frequently when the creditor needs immediate cash to purchase inventory. If you are the assignee, confirm that the debtor has no defenses for refusing to pay the creditor. In an assignment of rights, the assignee gets only the rights the assignor had; any defenses (excuses) the debtor has for not paying the assignor are also valid against the assignee. (This is in contrast to the situation when the assignee is a ***Holder in Due Course*** and may actually get better rights than the assignor held.)

2. Make certain that proper notice is given to the debtor if your company becomes the assignee of the right to collect money. Otherwise, if the debtor continues to pay the assignor you cannot force the debtor to make duplicate payments to your business. The only recourse is to try to recover from the assignor.

Sources of Information

1. The Internet Law Library provides information on contract law through *http://www.lawguru.com/lawlib/index.html*.

2. To learn more about assignment of rights, go to *http://fundamentals.westbuslaw.com*. Go to "Interactive Study Center" and scroll to Chapter 11, "Third Party Rights and Discharge."

Bб

Bailment Law

(For additional information, *see **Personal Property**.*)

Businesses today are involved in bailments in a variety of situations. A **bailment** is a relationship where the **bailor** (the owner of personal property) transfers temporary possession of the property to another party, the **bailee,** with the understanding the property is to be returned either to the owner or to a third party in substantially the same condition absent instructions to change the condition. Examples of bailments include a customer checking a coat in a restaurant; an accounting firm borrowing a stapler from the office next door; and a dry cleaning establishment taking a customer's coat for cleaning. The bailee may incur liability if the bailment property is changed or damaged. A bailment may be for a fee or gratuitous. As a general rule, the bailee must knowingly and willingly take possession of the property. (An exception exists in an **involuntary bailment**, which is discussed later.)

Types of Voluntary Bailments: The type of bailment is determined by which party benefits from the bailment relationship:

1. ***Bailment for the Sole Benefit of Bailor***
   Assume a homeowner is going on vacation and leaves her car in the driveway of her neighbor. The homeowner hands the car keys over to neighbor (the bailee) with the understanding the neighbor is not to drive the car during the homeown-

er's absence. This is a bailment for sole benefit of bailor (the homeowner).

2. *Bailment for the Sole Benefit of Bailee*

Assume the electricity goes out in a restaurant. The restaurant owner goes to the electronics store next door and borrows three large battery-operated lanterns. This is a bailment solely for the benefit of the bailee (the restaurant owner).

3. *Mutual Benefit Bailment*

In a mutual benefit bailment, both the bailor and the bailee receive some time of benefit. Assume a customer takes a roll of film to be developed to a photo shop. The customer/bailor receives the benefit of having her film developed and the photo shop/ bailee will receive compensation for the work of developing the film.

Involuntary Bailments: As mentioned previously, a bailment usually requires that the bailee knowingly and willingly accept possession of the bailment property. An exception exists when the property involved is *mislaid property*. When a person intentionally places an item of personal property in a location and then inadvertently leaves the personal property, it is considered mislaid. The owner or lessee of the site where the personal property is left becomes an involuntary bailee and has a duty of care toward the personal property.

Bailee's Duty of Care: In the past, courts held the bailee's duty of care depended on the type of bailment. For example, in a bailment for the sole benefit of the bailor, the bailee's duty involved taking minimal care of the property. Today most courts require the bailee take reasonable care of the property in all three types of voluntary bailments and in an involuntary bailment. What is considered reasonable care is addressed on a case-by-case basis.

Red Flag Situation

Situation: A customer in a local florist takes her wallet out to pay for roses. She forgets to remove the wallet from the counter and place it back in her purse. A florist employee sees the wallet but is too busy with another customer to place it safely away. A third party thief also sees the wallet and steals it. *Potential Problem:* An involuntary bailment existed when the florist employee knew (or should have known) the wallet was on the counter. As a result of her failure to take reasonable care of the wallet, the florist is liable to customer for the loss even though the customer was careless in leaving the wallet on the counter.

Special Categories of Bailments: The bailments discussed above are considered ordinary bailments. Two special categories of bailments involve *common carriers* and *innkeepers*.

1. ***Common carriers:*** A common carrier (one who is in the business of transporting goods for others) incurs a higher duty of care relevant to the bailment property. The common carrier is held to be strictly liable (the plaintiff does not have to prove negligence or intent) if goods are lost or damaged with narrow exceptions. The common carrier is not liable for loss or damage caused by an act of God; act of a public enemy; order of public authority; inherent nature of the goods; or act of the shipper of the goods.

2. ***Innkeepers:*** State laws limit the innkeeper's liability today. Most state statutes require that the innkeeper provide a safe for a guest's valuables and that the innkeeper inform guests of the availability and location of the safe. Many state laws limit the innkeeper's liability for goods not placed in the safe when proper notification was provided.

Red Flag Situation

Situation: A company executive attends an all-day seminar at a local restaurant. A valet for the restaurant parks her car in the restaurant parking lot. The executive leaves her new tablet computer in the trunk of the car. The car is stolen and the executive sues the restaurant for the loss of the car and the computer based on the bailee's duty to take reasonable care of the bailment property.

Potential Problem: In a voluntary bailment, the bailee is responsible for the care of the bailment property the bailee knowingly and willingly takes into possession. The restaurant knowingly and willing accepted possession of the car but was unaware of the computer in the trunk. The restaurant is therefore liable for the loss of the car but is not liable for loss of the computer.

Going Global

1. Bailment laws may differ in other countries. Companies involved in the servicing of personal property (such as electronic equipment) in other countries may be liable for the damage or loss of the bailment property.

2. Laws relating to liability of innkeepers for bailment property of guests vary in other countries. An innkeeper must strictly comply with any statutory requirements regarding the safekeeping of valuables.

Reducing Your Risks

1. Acquaint all employees with the duty of care that arises when a bailee agrees to take possession of bailment property.

2. Establish a policy for the safekeeping of mislaid property customers may leave in your place of business.

3. Avoid leaving valuables in the trunk of a car, in a coat pocket, or in any other place when the bailee is unaware of their existence.

Sources of Information

1. The law of bailments is discussed at the 'Lectric Law Library's web site at *http://www.lectlaw.com/def/b005.htm.*

2. More information on bailments is available at *http://www.swlearning.com/blaw/ fundamentals/fundamentals6e/fundamentals6e.html.* Click on "Interactive Study Center" and scroll to Chapter 28, "Personal Property and Bailments."

Bankruptcy Law

(For additional information, *see Financing Statement, Secured Transactions* and *Security Agreements.*)

The U. S. Constitution provides that Congress shall establish "...uniform Laws on the subject of Bankruptcies throughout the United States..." (Article I, Section 8) The Bankruptcy Code was substantially revised in 1978. The most recent revision is found in the Bankruptcy Abuse Prevention and Consumer Protection Act of 2005 (Senate Bill 256). *Bankruptcy law* serves two purposes: (1) the law provides the good-faith debtor an opportunity to start over and (2) the law makes certain the bankrupt's creditors of equal rank are treated in a fair and equitable manner. Bankruptcy law is based on federal statutes and hearings are conducted in federal bankruptcy courts. Bankruptcy proceedings incorporate relevant state laws applicable to liens, judgments, secured transactions, and exemptions.

Four main divisions in bankruptcy law (referred to as "chapters") are available to debtors. These are Chapters 7, 9, 11 and 13.

Chapter 7: A Chapter 7 bankruptcy proceeding is also referred to as "straight bankruptcy" or "liquidation." (11 U.S.C. § 7) In this proceeding, all of the debtor's nonexempt property is turned over to the bankruptcy trustee and sold at public auction. The sales proceeds are distributed to the creditors in order of preference as established by law. In the case of an individual debtor, all of the debtor's debts excluding nondischargeable debts are generally discharged. The Bankruptcy Abuse Prevention and Consumer Protection Act of 2005 provides significant changes relevant to an individual's filing for Chapter 7. The new law permits individual debtors to retain assets permitted under the debtor's state laws only if certain specific requirements are met. If the debtor is a partnership or corporation, the business entity may cease to exist according to applicable state law.

Chapter 7 relief is available to individuals and most business entities. Chapter 7 is not available for insurance companies, railroads, banks, savings and loan associations, credit unions, and investment companies licensed by the Small Business Administration.

When Chapter 7 is available and certain statutory requirements are met, the debtor may file a voluntary petition for relief or the creditors may file an involuntary petition. Charities and farmers are not subject to involuntary bankruptcy petitions. As a general rule, filing a Chapter 7 petition results in an automatic stay (freeze) on creditors' actions against the bankrupt. This stay means that a creditor can no longer begin or continue most lawsuits against the debtor relevant to the debt.

Red Flag Situation

Situation: A lumber company sells $20,000 in building supplies on credit to a local builder without having the debtor execute a *security agreement* and *financing statement*. The lumber company is therefore an unsecured creditor.

Potential Problem: As an unsecured general creditor, the lumber company is at the bottom of the list of unsecured creditors to be paid in case the builder files for Chapter 7 bankruptcy relief. Bankruptcy law establishes a priority list regarding payments to unsecured creditors. The first unsecured debts to be paid are administrative expenses (including court costs, attorney fees and trustee fees). Unsecured general creditors are ninth (and last) on the list. In many bankruptcy proceedings, there are no funds remaining to pay unsecured general creditors.

Chapter 11: Chapter 11 bankruptcy relief provides for reorganization. The relief is available to individuals (except commodities brokers and stockbrokers) and most business entities. The petition may be filed voluntarily by the debtor or the creditors may file an involuntary petition if certain statutory requirements are met. The debtor and creditors prepare and submit to the court a reorganization plan whereby the debtor will pay part of the outstanding debts and will be discharged from the rest of the debts. In most cases, the business continues in operation while it is in Chapter 11.

Red Flag Situation

Situation: A local lumber company receives notice that one of its customers, a construction company, has filed for Chapter 11 relief. The debtor owes the lumber company $20,000 for building supplies. The notice advises the creditor of a creditors' committee meeting but the creditor fails to attend the meeting.

Potential Problem: The debtor's reorganization plan is submitted to each class of creditors. The creditors may disapprove the plan if it adversely affects the class. After the creditors attending the meeting approved the plan, the owner of the construction company determines the plan adversely affects its rights. The plan has already been approved and confirmed by the court; the creditor therefore must accept the provisions of the plan.

Chapter 12: Chapter 12 relief is available to a family farmer, a partnership, or a closely held corporation that meets the statutory eligibility requirements regarding farming operations. The proceeding is voluntary only. The debtor submits a plan providing for repayment of debts for court approval. When all payments are made, the debtor is no longer liable for the dischargeable debts. In order to qualify for Chapter 12, the individual debtor must prove at least 50 percent of gross income depends on the farm operations and a minimum of 80 percent of outstanding debts are related to the farm.

If the farm family owns at least 50 percent of the debtor partnership or debtor closely held corporation that entity may qualify for Chapter 12 relief.

Chapter 13: Only individuals (including sole proprietors) with regular income and unsecured debts below a specific amount are eligible for Chapter 13 relief. The proceeding is voluntary only. The debtor submits a repayment plan for court approval. When all payments are made, the debtor is no longer liable for dischargeable debts.

Going Global

1. Bankruptcy laws vary greatly throughout the world. In certain cultures, bankruptcy is looked upon with great contempt and may be subject to criminal sanctions.

2. A major risk in selling on credit to foreign customers is the credit risk if the purchaser refuses to pay. Many sellers in the global marketplace utilize the documentary sale contract. The seller may then refuse to ship the goods until provided with an irrevocable promise from the buyer's bank that the bank will purchase the document (i.e., bill of lading) indicating title to the goods.

Reducing Your Risks

1. Become familiar with the various chapters of the Bankruptcy Code as they may impact your business both as a debtor and a creditor. Understand that the Bankruptcy Abuse Prevention and Consumer Protection Act of 2005 includes significant changes relevant to an individual's filing for Chapter 7 and Chapter 13 relief.

2. Make certain your company obtains a properly executed ***security agreement*** and files a ***financing statement*** in order to protect your interest in a debtor's collateral. Otherwise, you are considered an unsecured general creditor. If the debtor files for Chapter 7 relief, as unsecured general creditor you are at the bottom of the list of potential payees. In many cases, there is no money available to

pay this group.

3. Attend creditors' meetings when you receive notice a debtor has filed for bankruptcy relief in order to protect your interests and register any protest you may have for the proposed plan.

4. When your company receives court notice that a debtor has filed for bankruptcy, make certain the company's claim against the debtor is filed with the court in a timely manner. Failure to properly file a claim may result in losing the right to participate as a creditor.

5. If you are concerned about the solvency of one of your customers, consider accepting cash payments only. The filing of a bankruptcy petition results in a stay (freeze) on any actions by creditors.

Sources of Information

1. The American Bankruptcy Institute (ABI) provides extensive information on bankruptcy (including the Bankruptcy Abuse Prevention and Consumer Protection Act of 2005) at *http://www.abiworld.org*.

2. A complete copy of the federal Bankruptcy Code is available through Cornell University at *http://www.law.cornell.edu:80/uscode/11*.

3. To learn more, go to *http://www.swlearning.com/blaw/fundamentals/fundamentals6e/fundamentals6e.html*. Click on "Interactive Study Center" and go to Chapter 21, "Creditors Rights and Bankruptcy."

Battery

(For additional information, see *Torts*)

The intentional tort of **battery** occurs when the defendant (or an extension of the defendant, such as an umbrella) touches the plaintiff in a harmful or offensive manner without the consent of the plaintiff. (The tort of battery is different from the criminal activity defined as battery.) For the plaintiff to prevail in the tort action, the plaintiff must prove four elements:

1. the defendant (or an extension of defendant) intentionally touches plaintiff;

2. the plaintiff did not consent;

3. the touch is harmful or offensive to plaintiff; and

4. a person of normal sensibilities would consider the touching offensive.

Placing a harmful or offensive ingredient into a food, beverage or medication without plaintiff's consent can also be considered a battery.

The plaintiff has to prove the defendant intended the act that resulted in the battery; actual intent to harm is not required. Assume a supervisor, as a joke, tosses a sales manual at an employee and the employee suffers an eye injury. Although the supervisor did not intend to harm the employee, a battery has occurred.

When the Employer May Be Liable: According to agency law, the employer may be liable if an employee commits a tort "within the scope of employment." In the example above, the company may be liable for the supervisor's battery because it was committed "within the scope of employment."

Defenses Available in a Battery Claim: Potential defenses include consent; defense of oneself or other persons when real and apparent danger is present; and defense of property in certain situations if the force will not cause serious bodily harm or death.

Red Flag Situation

Situation: At a company party, a supervisor "spikes" the punch with an alcoholic beverage known to cause adverse reactions (including loss of vision) in some drinkers. Unaware of the alcohol, an employee drinks the punch and suffers partial blindness.

Potential Problem: The supervisor has committed a battery. According to agency law, the employer is also potentially liable since the battery was committed "within the scope of employment." (Many courts have ruled that torts occurring in connection with a company party are "within the scope of employment" because employees feel compelled to attend.)

Going Global

1. Tort law in certain other countries is similar to U.S. tort law. If a dependent agent (employee) of a U.S. company commits an act recognized as the tort of battery in another country, the employer may be liable.

2. In some countries, an action considered a tort (but not a crime) in the U. S. may be categorized as a crime in the host country.

Reducing Your Risks

1. Make certain employees understand that intentional torts do not require actual intent to harm on the defendant's part.

2. Understand the employer's potential tort liability if an employee commits a tort "within the scope of employment." Courts are regularly expanding the definition of

"scope of employment."

3. If your company operates overseas, review tort laws in the host country.

Sources of Information

1. For additional tort information, visit the Internet Law Library at *http://www.lawguru.com/ilawlib.*

2. More information is available at *http://www.swlearning.com/blaw/ fundamentals/fundamentals6e/fundamentals6e.html.* Click on "Interactive Study Center" and go to Chapter 4, "Torts and Cyber Torts."

•

Beneficiaries

(of Contractual Rights) (For more information, *see **Contracts.***)

According to contract law, a ***beneficiary*** is the party who receives the benefit of the agreement between the contracting parties. In a contract for insurance, for example, the insurer agrees to pay the party designated by the insured in the event of a loss. This designated party is the beneficiary of the contract between the insured and the insurance company. The beneficiary in an insurance policy may be the insured or a designated third party.

Contract law recognizes three categories of beneficiaries

1. *Creditor Beneficiary*
Assume a debtor owes a creditor $2000 on an outstanding debt. The debtor then sells his car to an auto buyer for $2000 with the understanding that the auto buyer will pay the money to the creditor to extinguish debtor's debt to creditor. The debtor has delegated to the auto buyer his duty to pay the $2000 owed to the creditor. The original creditor is considered the creditor beneficiary of the contract between the debtor and the auto buyer. As a general rule, delegation of the duty to pay a debt requires the permission of the original creditor.

The situation involving a creditor beneficiary arises when a buyer assumes an existing mortgage. Assume a homeowner still owes $40,000 on a mortgage to a finance company. The homeowner sells the home to a homebuyer. The finance company agrees to allow the homebuyer to assume the mortgage and the homebuyer will make the remaining payments on the mortgage. The finance company is considered the creditor beneficiary of the contract between the homeowner and the homebuyer.

Red Flag Situation

Situation: Homebuyer assumes Homeowner's existing mortgage. There are still ten years of payments remaining. After two years Homebuyer leaves the country and makes no further payments.

Potential Problem: Homeowner, as the original mortgagor, remains liable on the debt in the event Homebuyer defaults. When another party assumes an existing debt, the original debtor remains liable for nonpayment unless the original creditor agrees to release the original debtor from liability.

Donee Beneficiary

Assume a company offers to pay an artist for agreeing to paint a portrait of a retiring employee as the employee's retirement gift. In this case, the retiring employee, as the recipient of the gift, is considered the donee beneficiary of the contract between the company and the artist. If the artist breaches the contract by failing to paint the portrait, the employee may sue as the donee beneficiary.

The beneficiary named in an insurance policy is also considered a donee beneficiary.

Incidental Beneficiary

Assume the city has a contract with a construction company for the latter to repair certain city streets. The construction company fails to complete the repairs. A local furniture store's delivery truck is severely damaged due to a pothole the construction company failed to repair. As a user of the city streets, the furniture store is an incidental beneficiary to the contract between the city and the construction company. (In contrast, creditor and donee beneficiaries are intended beneficiaries.) As an incidental beneficiary, the furniture store cannot sue the construction company for breach of contract.

Going Global

Contract law varies from country to country. If one of your company's debtors abroad requests permission to delegate the duty to pay and another party will assume the debt, determine if the original party will also remain liable on the debt and confirm the creditworthiness of the party to whom the duty to pay is delegated.

Reducing Your Risks

1. Consider the risk involved when your company sells property and allows the new purchaser to assume your existing mortgage: if the new owner fails to pay, your company remains liable on the existing mortgage unless your mortgagee agreed to release your company from liability. If the value of the property is now less than the existing mortgage, your company may realize a significant loss by having to pay off the mortgage on property that has depreciated significantly in value. Make cer-

tain the mortgagee knows where to reach you and notifies you as soon as the new debtor misses a payment. If the mortgagee cannot reach you and must foreclose and sell the property at a loss, you (as original mortgagor) are still liable on the remaining debt.

2. If your company provides goods or services to third party donee beneficiaries, make certain personnel working with those beneficiaries understand the donee has the right to sue for breach of contract.

3. When a company's debtor asks to delegate its duty to pay to a third party, consider all risks involved. Confirm the new party's creditworthiness and make certain your company always has updated addresses for both parties.

Sources of Information

1. Additional information is available through Cornell Law School at *http://www.law.cornell.edu/topics/contracts*.html

2. To learn more, go to *http://www.swlearning.com/blaw/fundamentals/fundamentals6e/fundamentals6e.html*. Click on "Interactive Study Center" and go to Chapter 11, "Third Party Rights and Discharge."

Bona Fide Occupational Qualification

(For additional information, *see Age Discrimination, Americans with Disabilities Act* and *Civil Rights Act of 1964.*)

The term *bona fide occupational qualification (BFOQ)* refers to one of several defenses available to an employer charged with employment discrimination. The BFOQ defense may apply when an employer requires certain qualifications in order for an employee to perform the job. Assume a movie director is interviewing applicants for the lead role in a movie based on the life of King George. A female actress is turned down and charges gender discrimination. The director can claim that requiring a male play the lead role is a bona fide occupational qualification.

Red Flag Situation

Situation: A movie director is interviewing applicants for the lead role in a movie based on the life of Queen Anne. The director states only Caucasian females will be considered for the job, claiming this requirement is a bona fide occupational qualification.

Potential Problem: The defense of bona fide occupational qualification is not a viable defense to claims of race discrimination.

Going Global

The bona fide occupational qualification defense applies to complaints of U.S. citizens working abroad for a company under the control of an American employer.

Reducing Your Risks

1. Be familiar with the latest regulations and decisions relevant to the bona fide occupational qualification defense. This information is available through the Equal Employment Opportunity Commission.

2. Remember that the bona fide occupational qualification defense does not apply to claims of race discrimination.

Sources of Information

1. Information on defenses available to employers charged with employment discrimination is provided by the federal Equal Employment Opportunity Commission at *http://www.eeoc.gov.*

2. The federal Department of Labor provides information on defenses available for discrimination claims at *http://www.dol.gov.*

3. The International Labor Organization's web site includes information on employment discrimination in other countries at *http://www.ilo.org.*

4. To learn more, visit *http://www.swlearning.com/blaw/fundamentals/fundamentals6e/fundamentals6e.html.* Click on "Interactive Study Center" and go to Chapter 23, "Employment Law."

Bribery

(For additional information, *see Foreign Corrupt Practices Act.*)

The crime of *bribery* occurs when the bribing party offers something of value to another party in exchange for a favor and the offer violates a criminal statute. Categories of bribery include: (1) commercial bribery; (2) bribery of a public official; and (3) bribery of a foreign official. Bribery may violate a state criminal law and/or a federal criminal law. The crime occurs when the bribe is offered, even if the offeree refuses to accept the bribe. Acceptance of a bribe is considered a separate criminal offense.

Elements of a Bribe: According to criminal law, a conviction for any crime requires two elements: (1) the defendant committed the prohibited act as defined in the statute (or in some cases, omitted to perform a required act, such as paying taxes) and

(2) the defendant had the required state of mind (mens rea) as defined by the statute. Conviction for bribery therefore requires: (1) the defendant offered a bribe as defined by the state or federal criminal statute and (2) the defendant had the required intent (state of mind) as defined by the applicable statute.

Assume a sales representative for a major food supply company offers a cash amount to the purchasing agent of a restaurant chain if the purchasing agent will make certain the sales representative's company gets a contract with the chain. As soon as the sales representative makes the offer, the crime of commercial bribery has been committed.

Red Flag Situation

Situation: In the above example, assume the purchasing agent refused to accept the money and the sales representative assumes no law has been broken. *Potential Problem:* The crime of bribery is committed when the offer is made. If the other party refuses to take the offer, the party making the offer is still criminally liable. Accepting a bribe is a separate crime.

Commercial Bribes and Trade Secrets: A major concern in today's business world involves commercial bribes offered in exchange for a trade secret. Examples of trade secrets may range from customer lists to a secret recipe for a restaurant chain's barbeque sauces.

Bribery of Public Officials: As mentioned, another category of bribes involves public officials. Assume a local school board will soon determine which food supplier will be awarded the contract for supplying food to the local school cafeterias. The salesperson for a food supply company offers a school board member cash in exchange for the board member's favorable vote. In this situation, the salesperson has committed the crime of bribery of a public official.

Gift Giving: Another potential problem for businesses involves gift giving. When a business gives a gift to another party who is in a position to convey a favor on the donor, there is the risk of the gift being interpreted as a bribe. For this reason, many U.S. businesses restrict the practice of gift giving.

Red Flag Situation

Situation: A salesperson for a major computer manufacturing firm sends an expensive birthday gift to the owner of an electronics store. *Potential Problem:* The gift may be construed as a bribe given in order for the salesperson to obtain a future sales contract with the store.

Bribery of Foreign Officials: The major federal legislation addressing bribery of a foreign official is the U. S. Foreign Corrupt Practices Act (FCPA), which is more fully addressed in a separate topic.

Going Global

1. The FCPA, which prohibits U.S. businesses and businesspersons from offering bribes to foreign officials and candidates for foreign office in exchange for business advantages, applies to U.S. businesses of all sizes, including sole proprietorships and entrepreneurs. Violation of the FCPA carries heavy penalties. A business can face up to $2 million in fines. Individuals convicted under the FCPA face personal liability up to $100,000 and up to five years in prison.

2. Bribery laws differ from country to country. In some areas of the world, conviction for bribery may carry the death penalty.

Reducing Your Risks

1. Become familiar with the federal laws on bribery as well as the laws in the state(s) where your business operates.

2. Understand that a bribe occurs when the bribe is offered, even if the other party declines the offer. A party who accepts the bribe has committed a separate crime.

3. Be aware the bribe can consist of anything that may be of value to another party; cash is only one medium of bribery.

4. Prior to entering a foreign market, consult with an attorney familiar with the criminal laws of the host country; an action not considered a bribe in the home country might be a bribe abroad.

5. Regularly review the latest court decisions relevant to the Foreign Corrupt Practices Act.

6. If your company does not yet have a Code of Ethics, consider adopting one as soon as possible. Include in the Code your company's policy on gift giving. Surveys show that employees prefer working for a company with a clearly defined Code of Ethics to help them address "gray" areas that may lead to illegal practices.

7. A provision of the new federal Sarbanes-Oxley Act mandates that certain businesses have a confidential system whereby concerned parties (including employees) can report unethical and illegal accounting and auditing practices. Briberies disguised as legitimate business deductions could be reported through this system. Make certain that your business is in compliance. One approach is the use of a web-based reporting system. Additional information is available through the Corporate Governance Web site at *http://www.corpgov.net*. (For more information on this Act, *see* H.R. 3762.)

Sources of Information

1. The criminal codes of various states can be accessed online through *http://www.findlaw.com*.

2. Additional information on the Foreign Corrupt Practices Act is provided by the U.S. Department of Justice at *http://www.usdoj.gov*.

3. For information on your state's criminal laws, go to *http://www.findlaw.com*. Then proceed to "State", select your state under "Laws: Cases/Codes."

4. To learn more, go to *http://www.swlearning.com/blaw/fundamentals/fundamentals6e/fundamentals6e.html*. Click on "Interactive Study Center" and go to Chapter 3, "Ethics and Social Responsibility."

Cc

Civil Rights Act of 1964 (Title VII)

(For additional information, *see Age Discrimination, Americans with Disability Act* and *Sexual Harassment*.)

The major federal law addressing employment discrimination is *Title VII of the Civil Rights Act of 1964*. (42 U.S.C. §§ Sections 2000 e – 2000 e-17) The law applies to businesses engaged in interstate commerce (commerce between the states or between one state and a foreign country or an Indian tribe) that have fifteen or more employees. The law also applies to labor unions with hiring halls, labor unions with fifteen or more employees, employment agencies and state and local agencies. Discrimination based on sex, religion, race, color or national origin is prohibited in all phases of the employment process including interviewing, retirement benefits, and termination. Prior to filing a lawsuit based on Title VII, the complainant must first file a complaint and seek a ruling from the federal Equal Employment Opportunity Commission (EEOC). Businesses that are not covered by the federal law are still subject to the employment discrimination laws in the states in which they operate.

Intentional and Unintentional Discrimination: Title VII categorizes discrimination as intentional or unintentional. Intentional discrimination on the part of the employer is referred to as "disparate-treatment discrimination." Assume a transportation company determines that no females will be hired as truck drivers. A qualified female driver applies for a job and is turned down based on the company policy. This is an example of intentional sexual discrimination.

Unintentional discrimination is referred to as "disparate-impact discrimination."

Assume the accounting department at the transportation company requires all applicants for positions as cost accountants either have experience in cost accounting or have taken at least one course in the subject. Although the county's population is 53 percent female, only five percent meet these qualifications. This is an example of unintentional discrimination. In this case, the employer may successfully defend its requirements based on business necessity.

Defenses to Title VII Claims: The law recognizes three defenses available to employers charged with Title VII discrimination: business necessity, bona fide occupational qualification, and seniority system.

1. ***Business Necessity.*** In the example cited above, the transportation company may successfully defend itself against a sexual discrimination claim by showing that the requirements relating to cost accounting are necessary for an employee to properly perform the job.

2. ***Bona Fide Occupational Qualification.*** This defense is available when a certain trait is required for job performance. For example, a bridal magazine may hire only females to model wedding gowns. (For additional information, see the topic titled ***Bona Fide Occupational Qualification***.)

3. ***Seniority System.*** Assume the transportation company has a promotion policy based on seniority. A male employee has been with the company 15 years while a female employee was hired six months ago. Both apply for a promotion to a newly created position within their department. The male gets the position based on his seniority and the female employee claims sexual discrimination. The company has a viable defense provided its seniority system is fair and equitable.

Red Flag Situation

Situation: A local restaurant is open seven days a week. Each employee works six days per week. One employee requests that he be allowed to take his day off on Wednesday for religious reasons. (Wednesday is a very slow day at the restaurant.) The restaurant manager refuses the request, saying the employee must take Mondays off.

Potential Problem: The employee may claim discrimination based on his religion. According to Title VII, the employer has the duty to "reasonably accommodate" an employee's religious practices provided the accommodation is not an undue hardship for the business. In this case, allowing the employee to take Wednesdays off would not be an undue hardship.

Going Global

1. Title VII of the Civil Rights Act of 1964 applies abroad when the complainant is an American citizen and the company is under the control of an American employer. Defenses available in claims filed abroad include:

   a. ***Foreign Compulsion Defense***
   This defense applies when enforcement of a U.S. law violates the host country's laws.

   b. ***Bona Fide Occupational Qualification (BFOQ)***
   See above for a discussion of the BFOQ defense.

2. Some countries have pro-discrimination laws that forbid an employer from hiring employees of certain national origins or religions; for example, employing females is forbidden in certain parts of the world.

Reducing Your Risks

1. Review job announcements carefully prior to publication for any language that may be construed as discriminatory as to sex, religion, race, color or national origin.

2. Be familiar with the current EEOC regulations and the latest guidelines regarding questions that are considered illegal in the interview process.

3. Be familiar with your state's employment discrimination laws; both state and federal discrimination laws may apply to your business.

4. If your company is in control of operations abroad, remember that Title VII applies to U.S. citizens working in the operation.

Sources of Information

1. Information on Title VII is available through the federal Equal Employment Opportunity Commission at *http://www.eeoc.gov*.

2. Discrimination issues relating to employers are available at the federal Department of Labor's web site at *http://www.dol.gov*.

3. Information on an individual state's employment discrimination laws are available through the web site of the state's Office of Attorney General.

4. For information on discrimination in other countries, visit the International Labor Organization site at *http://www.ilo.org*.

5. To learn more, go to *http://www.swlearning.com/blaw/fundamentals/fundamentals6e/fundamentals6e.html.* Click on "Interactive Study Center" and go to Chapter 23, "Employment Law."

Clayton Act

(For additional information on antitrust laws, *see **Sherman Act**.*)

In order to expand the regulation of anticompetitive practices established by the Sherman Act, Congress passed the ***Clayton Act***. While the Sherman Act's main focus is on monopolization and attempts to monopolize, the Clayton Act focuses on business activities that may harm competition. Activities regulated by the Clayton Act include: tying agreements; price discrimination; exclusive dealing contracts; requirements contracts; interlocking directorates; and mergers and acquisitions.

Per Se Violations and the Rule of Reason. Certain activities regulated by the Clayton Act have been determined to be illegal per se (illegal in itself) by the courts. Price fixing falls into this category. In this situation, the activity is deemed automatically illegal and the injured plaintiff is not required to provide detailed evidence of the unreasonableness of the activity.

When the rule of reason is applied, the court will analyze the restrictive effect on competition vis-à-vis any business justification to determine the overall impact. The courts apply the rule of reason to mergers and acquisitions.

Going Global

1. The European equivalent of U.S. antitrust laws is referred to as "competition laws."

2. While U.S. antitrust laws provide for court interpretation, Germany's competition law is very detailed and allows little discretion on the court's part.

3. Anti-competition practices within the European Union are regulated according to Articles 81 and 82 of the Treaty of Rome.

4. According to the European Union Merger Regulation, parties to any business combination that will have a "community dimension" must file for approval with the Commission of the European Communities prior to the transaction.

Reducing Your Risks

1. When considering a merger or acquisition of another company, have counsel familiar with antitrust laws review the proposal for possible antitrust violations.

2. Avoid dictating what other parties must charge when selling your goods or services; price fixing is illegal per se.

3. U. S. businesses are subject to both state and federal antitrust laws. The area of antitrust law is complex and violations are subject to heavy penalties. Many businesses find they have unknowingly broken the law. It is therefore advisable that decision-makers become acquainted with those practices that may be deemed anticompetitive.

Sources of Information

1. Provision and guidelines relative to the U.S. antitrust laws are available from the Antitrust Division of the U. S. Department of Justice at *http://www.usdoj.gov*. Go to "Search" and type in "Antitrust Laws".

2. Summaries of recent antitrust cases are available at *http://www.stolaf.edu/people/becker/antitrust/index.htm*.

3. The U.S. Federal Trade Commission provides a primer on antitrust at *http://www.ftc.gov/bc/compguide/antitrust.htm*.

Close Corporation

(For additional information, *see **Corporation**.*)

Close Corporation: The term ***close corporation*** refers to a corporation owned and controlled by a small number of shareholders. Sometimes referred to as a "family corporation," the entity's number of shareholders is determined by state statute. Many states permit a close corporation to operate without many of the formalities required for larger corporations.

Red Flag Situation

1. ***Situation:*** A local florist operates as a close corporation with seven shareholders. The shareholders are members of the same family. Due to a family disagreement on a totally different matter, four of the shareholders decide to block any recommendations of the other three. According to the by-laws, passage of any proposal requires only a simple majority approval.
   Potential Problem: As a result of the small number of shareholders in a close corporation, it may be quite easy for a simple majority to dictate all corporate policy and thereby freeze out the other shareholders unless the bylaws require more than a simple majority to approve a vote.

Going Global

Corporate laws vary from country to country. Some countries do not have provisions for a close corporation. In other countries, the number of allowable shareholders varies and the formalities required must be satisfied.

Reducing Your Risks

1. Review the requirements for a close corporation in your own state; the number of

allowable shareholders varies.

2. When considering whether to become a shareholder in a close corporation, carefully review the attributes of the other shareholders. Make certain that you can work with them and they share your ideas as to the goals and objectives of the corporation.

Sources of Information

1. For information on your state's corporation laws, refer to Cornell University at *http://www.law.cornell.edu/topics/state_statutes.html*.

2. Additional information on corporate law is available from the University of Cincinnati College of Law at *http://www.law.uc.edu/CCL*.

3. To learn more about corporate ownership in other countries, go to the World Trade Organization site at *http://www.wto.org*.

4. Additional information is available at *http://www.swlearning.com/blaw/fundamentals/fundamentals6e/fundamentals6e.html*. Click on "Interactive Study Center" and go to Chapter 25, "Corporate Formation, Financing, and Termination."

Computer Software Copyright Act

(For additional information, *see Copyrights*.)

The federal *Computer Software Copyright Act (CSCA)* was implemented in 1980 as an amendment to the Copyright Act of 1976. The purpose of the CSCA was to categorize computer programs as "literary works" and thereby protect the programs from copyright infringements. According to the CSCA, a protected program is a "set of statements or instructions to be used directly or indirectly in a computer in order to bring about a certain result."

Application of the CSCA: The courts are inconsistent in their rulings as to whether certain aspects of computer programs can be protected by copyright. Several courts have ruled that protection goes to those parts of the program that can be read only by a computer (i.e., binary-language object codes) as well as to those portions readable by a human being.

The issue of whether other aspects of a program such as menus, general appearance and command structure can be protected has not been consistently determined.

Red Flag Situation

Situation: A major software company develops a new computer game for children. Recognizing the popularity of a competitor's newest game, the company incorporates the competitor's general appearance and command structure into its own game. The competitor's program is copyrighted.

Potential Problem: The courts are inconsistent on their rulings relevant to whether the "look and feel" aspects of computer programs are copyrightable. In some jurisdictions, the court may determine the software company infringed on the competitor's copyright by incorporating the general appearance and command structure into its own game.

Going Global

Foreign copyright laws vary from country to country. Works considered copyrightable in one country may not be recognized as copyrightable in another country. In addition, existing copyright laws are not vigorously enforced in certain countries.

Reducing Your Risks

1. If your company develops computer software programs, make certain the programs are protected by U.S. copyright laws and applicable foreign copyright laws. In the U.S., a party cannot sue for copyright infringement unless the complainant has a copyright on the work.

2. Seek legal advice from attorneys familiar with domestic and international copyright laws to protect your software program from infringement at home and abroad. The area of intellectual property law is very complex and the services of attorneys specializing in this area can be invaluable.

3. Make certain your computer programmers understand the risks of infringing on a competitor's copyright relative to various elements of the program such as sequence, structure, and organization. These are some of the elements of a program that may be protected by copyright.

4. Various aspects of the Copyright Software Protection Act are still being interpreted by the courts. Consult with an attorney on a regular basis if your business in engaged in software development.

Sources of Information

1. The U.S. Copyright Office provides extensive information on the Copyright Software Protection Act at *http://www.copyright.gov*.

2. U.S. Supreme Court decisions on copyright issues are available through Cornell

University at *http://www.law.cornell.edu/topics/copyright.html.*

3. Copyright information is available from the Cyberspace Law Institute at *http://www.cli.org.*

4. Information on the North Atlantic Free Trade Agreement (NAFTA) provision on international copyright protection is available at *http://www.nafta.org.*

5. To learn more about international intellectual property rights, visit the World Trade Office at *http://www.wto.org.*

6. Additional information is available at *http://www.swlearning.com/blaw/fundamentals/fundamentals6e/fundamentals6e.html.* Click on "Interactive Study Center" and go to Chapter 4, "Torts and Cyber Torts" and Chapter 5, "Intellectual Property and Internet Law."

Conditions to a Contract

A defense to a breach of contract claim may be the existence of ***conditions to a contract***. These conditions include: (1) a condition precedent, which is a condition that must be met before a contracting party is required to perform and (2) a condition subsequent, which is a condition which occurs after the contract begins and relieves a party from the duty to continue performance.

Assume a retail chain agrees to buy five acres of land for a new store provided the buyer can obtain a loan of $300,000 at a maximum fixed interest rate of six percent. The potential buyer is unable to obtain a loan under eight percent. The agreement to purchase the land included a condition precedent. Since the retailer was unable to obtain the required loan, the company is relieved of its duty to buy the land.

In another situation, an employee agrees to work in a retailer's bookkeeping department until the employee becomes a licensed Certified Public Accountant (CPA). The employee passes the examinations and becomes a CPA. The employee is then relieved of the duty to continue working for the retailer. This is an example of a condition subsequent.

Red Flag Situation

Situation: An employee with a five-year contract with your company announces she is leaving. You immediately consult an attorney and plan to file a breach of contract lawsuit against the employee.

Potential Problem: If the employment contract included a condition subsequent and that condition has been met, the employee is no longer required to work for your company.

Going Global

1. Contract laws vary from one country to another. If your company plans to enter into an international contract that contains a condition, make certain the condition is recognized according to the laws of the host country.

2. Some countries require a writing in order for certain contracts to be enforceable. When entering into an international contract that includes a condition, make certain the contract is in writing if the applicable law requires a writing.

Sources of Information

1. Additional contract information is available from Cornell Law School at *http://www.law.cornell.edu/topics/contracts.html.*

2. To learn more, visit *http://www.swlearning.com/blaw/fundamentals/fundamentals6e/fundamentals6e.html.* Click on "Interactive Study Center" and go to Chapter 11, "Third Party Rights and Discharge."

Consumer Credit Protection Act

Congress passed the ***Consumer Credit Protection Act of 1968*** (the Act) to protect consumers in credit transactions. The Act (15 U.S.C. 1601 - 1693r) requires creditors to disclose the cost of credit in an easy-to-comprehend manner (truth in lending). The Act, which established the National Commission on Consumer Finance, is frequently referred to as the Truth-in-Lending Act. It has been amended by the Fair Credit Billing Act; Fair Credit Reporting Act; Fair Credit Debt Collection Act; and the Equal Credit Opportunity Act. The Act was also amended in 1978 by the Electronic Fund Transfer Act (EFTA) to regulate the use of electronic fund transfers.

In addition to compliance with federal consumer credit laws, U.S. businesses are subject to state consumer laws.

Red Flag Situation

Situation: A local car dealer shows a new car to a prospective buyer. The dealer presents the buyer with a loan application whereby the car dealership will finance the sale at a stated interest rate. The buyer mentions that she is single. Based on this information, she is denied credit.

Potential Problem: The dealer has violated the Equal Credit Opportunity Act (an amendment to the Consumer Credit Protection Act) by discriminating against the buyer based on marital status.

Going Global

Some countries are very protective of consumers in credit transactions while other countries have no consumer credit laws. Be familiar with the consumer credit laws in the host country prior to entering into a consumer transaction there.

Reducing Your Risks

1. If your company is engaged in the extension of credit, be familiar with the various state and federal laws protecting consumers.

2. Review your loan application forms for possible violation of consumer protection laws.

3. Make certain employees involved in credit transactions are familiar with the legal restrictions on questions the creditor can legally ask.

Sources of Information

1. Guidelines on consumer protection in credit transactions are available from the Federal Reserve at *http://www.federalreserve.gov/pubs/consumerhdbk*.

2. Information on federal statutes, court decisions and state statutes relative to consumer credit is available at *http://www.law.cornell.edu/topics/consumer_credit.html*.

3. More information is available at *http://www.swlearning.com/blaw/fundamentals/fundamentals6e/fundamentals6e.html*. Click on "Interactive Study Center" and go to Chapter 19, "Checks, Banking, and Cyberbanking."

Constitutional Law

(For additional information, *see **Interstate Commerce Clause**.*)

Constitutional Law: The area of law based on either a state constitution or the U.S. Constitution is referred to as ***constitutional law***. The U. S. Constitution is considered the supreme law of the land and will prevail in case of a conflict with a state constitution.

Contract

A ***contract*** is an agreement between two or more parties. In order to be enforceable in a court of law, the agreement must meet certain legal requirements and be in the proper form.

Categories of Contracts: Contracts may be categorized in several different ways.

1. *Categories based on enforceability*

A *valid contract* meets all of the legal requirements and is enforceable by either party in court.

A *void contract* is unenforceable by either party. Void contracts include contracts that are illegal (such as contracts to commit a crime or a tort) and contracts entered into by a person who has been declared insane by a court and has a court-appointed guardian. Courts have a "hands off" attitude toward void contracts.

A *voidable contract* is a contract where one or both parties have the power to avoid their contractual duties. If they do not choose to avoid the contract, it is enforceable. A contract entered into by a minor is voidable on the minor's part until the minor reaches the age of 18 and for a reasonable time thereafter.

Assume a retailer sells a television set to a sixteen-year-old buyer. The buyer, as a minor, has the power to avoid the contract until reaching the age of 18 and for a reasonable time after reaching that age. If the minor chooses to avoid the contract, the minor can demand the return of the purchase money. Many states require she return the television if the minor still has it in possession.

Contracts entered into by parties under the influence of drugs or alcohol and by parties who are temporarily insane (but have not been adjudicated insane) are also voidable by the party who is under the influence or who is temporarily insane.

An *unenforceable contract* has all of the elements required for a valid contract but for another reason cannot be enforced. For example, a verbal contract that meets all of the requirements for a valid contract may be unenforceable because it is not in writing. Each state has a *Statute of Frauds* that requires certain contracts must be in writing to be enforceable. For additional information on which contracts to be in writing, see the topic *Statute of Frauds*.

2. *Categories Based on Stage of Completion*

An *executory contract* is a contract where one or both parties have not yet performed their contractual duties.

An *executed contract* is a contract where both parties have fully performed.

3. *Categories Based on Number of Promises*

In a *unilateral contract*, a promise is exchanged for an act. Assume an attorney promises an artist $400 if the latter will paint a mural on the wall of the reception room of the law office. This is a unilateral contract. If the artist does not paint the mural, the artist is not liable for breach of contract.

A *bilateral contract* involves the exchange of two promises. Assume an attorney promises an artist $400 if the latter will promise to paint a mural for the law office and the artist gives the required promise. If the mural is not painted, the artist is liable for breach of contract.

Red Flag Situation

Situation: A dress shop sells a $1500 graduation gown to a seventeen year old. The minor wears the dress to the graduation dance and returns the used (and dirty) dress the next day and demands her money back.

Potential Problem: Because the buyer is a minor, the contract is voidable on the minor's part. The latter has the power to avoid the contract and demand her money back.

(Some states now require the minor to compensate for damage to the goods; other states do not.)

Required Elements of a Contract. A valid contract must have the following elements:

1. *Agreement*
   The agreement consists of an offer (made by the offeror) and an acceptance (by the offeree).

Requirements for a valid offer

   a. Offeror's intent: In determining whether the offeror intended to make an offer, the courts apply an objective test (whether an objective third party would conclude a serious offer was made).

   b. Communication of the offer to the offeree.

   c. Offer is sufficiently clear and complete to enable a court to form a remedy in case of breach.

Duration of Offers

Generally, the offeror can revoke (terminate) the offer any time until the offeree accepts. Two exceptions to this general rule involve: (1) option contracts, where the offeree pays to keep the option to accept open and (2) a firm offer made in writing and signed by a merchant seller where the seller promises the offer will remain open for a specified period of time.

Termination of Offer

An offer is terminated by the following means:

   a. rejection of the offer by the offeree;

   b. death or incapacitation of either party;

c. destruction of the specific subject matter of the offer;

d. the offer becomes illegal due to a statute or court decision; and

e. time specified in the offer passes. If the offer did not specify a time limit, termination of offer occurs after a reasonable period of time.

2. *Consideration*

Courts refer to **consideration** as "legal detriment." Consideration is present when (a) a party promises to perform an act or performs an act the party had no prior duty to do or (b) a party promises to refrain from or refrains from an act the party had a legal right to perform.

Courts do not recognize "past consideration" as valid. Assume a retailer tells a store salesperson, "Because you did such a good job for the store last month, I will add a $200 bonus to your paycheck next week." The bonus is not included and the salesperson sues. The plaintiff cannot enforce the promise of the bonus because the salesperson had given the consideration (work performed the previous month) before the retailer made the promise to pay the bonus.

Exceptions to the consideration requirement:

a. When a party who has had debts discharged in bankruptcy gives a former creditor a new promise to pay the discharged debt and the bankruptcy court approves, the new promise is enforceable.

b. When the legal theory of **promissory estoppel** applies. Those jurisdictions which recognize this theory require the following:

i. Promisor makes a promise with the reasonable expectation the other party will rely on the promise;

ii. The other party justifiably relies on the promise; and

iii. The other party suffers consequences as a result of the reliance.

3. *Genuine Assent*

Genuine assent exists when a party voluntarily enters into a contract with full knowledge of the terms. Lack of assent may be based on undue influence; duress; fraudulent misrepresentation; mistake; or unconscionability.

- Undue influence exists when a party agrees to a contract due to the excessive influence of the other party.

- Duress exists when a party enters into a contract due to threats of harm by the other party.

- Four elements are required for fraudulent misrepresentation to occur: (i) the defendant misrepresented a material fact; (ii) with intent to deceive; (iii) the victim justifiably relied on the misrepresentation; and (iv) due to the justifiable reliance, the victims suffered damages.

- A mistake may be unilateral or bilateral. As a general rule, a unilateral mistake does not allow the mistaken party to disaffirm the contract unless the other party knew or should have known of the mistake and took unfair advantage of it. A bilateral mistake regarding a material fact allows either party to disaffirm the contract.

- Unconscionability exists when the parties are not in equal bargaining position and the party holding the most power takes unfair advantage of the weaker party.

4. *Capacity*

Both parties must have legal capacity to contract. Lack of capacity may be based on minority (under eighteen years of age); being under the influence of drugs or alcohol; or insanity.

As mentioned earlier, as a general rule a contract entered by a minor is voidable. An exception exists when the contract was for "necessaries" for the minor. In that case, the minor must pay reasonable value for the goods or services.

5. *Legality*

In order to be valid, a contract must be for a legal purpose. A contract is illegal if it (1) violates a statute or (2) violates a public policy. Statutes that render a contract illegal include closing laws; usury laws; gambling laws, and laws that require licenses or permits when the license or permit is to protect the public.

Contracts violating public policy include contracts to commit torts, certain contracts with covenants not to compete, and contracts with exculpatory (hold harmless) clauses.

As a general rule, contracts in restraint of trade are illegal. One exception involves *covenants not to compete* when certain requirements are met. Today employment contracts frequently contain a covenant not to compete in the event the employee leaves the job. The covenant must meet the reasonableness test. To satisfy the test, the employer must demonstrate the covenant is reasonably necessary to protect the business interest of the employer and the agreement is reasonable as to geographic area and time. State laws vary on requirements and enforcibility of these covenants.

Covenants not to compete are also included in a contract to sell a business. In this situation, the seller agrees not to compete with the new owner of the business. If the buyer pays extra for the goodwill of the business, the time span and geographic area may be extended and still meet the reasonableness test.

Red Flag Situation

Situation: An accountant agrees to work for an accounting firm for two years. When the two years are up, the accountant leaves the firm. Five years later the accountant opens a competing firm across town. The former employer sues based on a covenant not to compete which provided the accountant would not set up a competing firm or work for a competitor for 20 years within the city limits. The accountant claims this is an unreasonable restriction.

Potential Problem: A court may agree with that the covenant is unreasonable as to time and allow the accountant to open a competing firm.

A contract may contain an exculpatory clause ("hold harmless" clause) where one party agrees it will not hold the other party liable for any injuries even if due to the negligence of the second party. As a general rule, the courts will not enforce these clauses. An exception is when both parties to the contract hold equal bargaining power and fully understand the clause.

Proper Form: An enforceable contract must contain the elements mentioned above and also be in the proper form. As mentioned previously, the Statute of Frauds requires that certain contracts be in writing in order to be enforceable. For a discussion of those contracts that must be in writing, see the *Statute of Frauds* topic.

Going Global

1. Laws vary in different countries as to which contracts must in be writing. Prior to entering into a verbal contract with a party in another country, make certain the verbal contract will be enforceable abroad.

2. The United Nations Convention on Contracts for the International Sale of Goods (CISG) addresses international sales contracts for commercial goods. Parties may "opt out" and choose which law to apply in case a dispute arises.

Reducing Your Risks

1. Never enter into a contract without fully understanding all the terms. Beware of any situation where the other party tries to rush you into an agreement. In an equitable situation, the other party will want to make sure you understand the contract.

2. The safest approach is to require a writing even if the contract does not come under the Statute of Frauds. This can avoid later disputes as to each party's understanding of the terms of the contract.

3. Understand that if the other party lacks capacity to contract, that party has the power to avoid the contract.

4. If you are selling goods (tangible, movable property), review Article 2 of the Uniform Commercial Code. Article 2 explains how certain terms in a contract for the sale of goods can be left blank (such as price, time, and place of delivery) and the Code will "fill in the blanks" for you in a manner that may not be satisfactory to you.

5. Prior to signing an important contract, have competent counsel review it to avoid any "surprises" at a later time.

6. If you plan to use form contracts in your business, have them reviewed by counsel to make certain they meet the requirements for enforceability.

7. If you are involved in contracts for the international sale of goods, become familiar with the provisions of the CISG.

Sources of Information

1. Additional information is available at the following site: *http://www.law.cornell.edu/topics/contracts.html.*

2. To access information on the Uniform Commercial Code in your state, go to *http://www.law.cornell.edu.* Select your state and then select "Commercial Code."

3. To learn more about the CISG, visit *http://www.cisg.law.pace.edu/cisg/text/treaty.html.*

4. Additional information is available at *http://www.swlearning.com/blaw/fundamentals/fundamentals6e/fundamentals6e.html.* Click on "Interactive Study Center" and go to Chapter 7, "Nature and Classification."

Copyright

(For additional information, *see Computer Software Protection Act.*)

Historical Background: The U. S. Constitution provides Congress shall have the power "to promote Progress of Science and useful Arts, by securing for limited Times to Authors and Inventors the exclusive Right to their respective Writings and Discoveries." (Article I, Section 8) Based on this Constitutional provision, Congress passed laws to protect copyrights and patents.

A ***copyright*** is a legal right in intellectual property available to creators of certain works that gives the holder exclusive right to sell or use the material for a specified time.

Works That Can Be Copyrighted: Among the works that can be copyrighted are literature; music; dramas; pictures; audiovisual works; graphics and sculptures; sound recordings; computer software; pantomimes; dance choreographies; menus; product packaging; and architectural plans. The Copyright Act of 1976 was amended by the *Computer Software Protection Act* to now provide copyright protection for computer software programs.

In order to receive copyright protection the material must be contained in a durable medium of communication. (Ideas cannot therefore be copyrighted.) Copyrights for works created after January 1, 1978 are valid for the life of the creator plus 70 years. If a publishing house owns the copyright, the right is good for 95 years from publication date or 120 years from creation date, whichever is shorter.

Red Flag Situations

1. *Situation:* A major retail chain includes an area where videos are shown to children while their parents shop.
   Potential Problem: If the chain has not paid the "umbrella fee" to the Motion Pictures Licensing Corporation (MPLC), the business can be liable for copyright infringement.

2. *Situation:* An insurance company plays "music on hold" while customers are waiting for the next available sales representative to answer the telephone call.
   Potential Problem: If the company has not paid the "umbrella fee" to the Association for Composers and Producers of Music (ASCAP), the company can be liable for copyright infringement.

Registration of Copyrights: A copyright is registered with the U.S. Copyright Office in Washington, D.C. On-line forms are available from the U.S. Copyright Office at *http://www.loc.gov/copyright.* An author cannot sue for infringement unless the material was registered.

When Material Can Be Copied Without Infringement: The Copyright Act provides a narrow exception allowing a party to copy protected material without infringing. This "Fair Use Exception" permits reproducing protected material for certain purposes including "…criticism, comment, news reporting, teaching…scholarship or research…" (Section 107) In determining whether the reproduction for one of these purposes comes under the fair use exception, the Act considers:

1. the purpose and character of the use, including whether such use is of a commercial nature or is for a nonprofit educational purpose;

2. the nature of the copyright work;

3. the amount and substantiality of the portion used in relation to the copyrighted

work as a whole; and

4. the effect of the use upon the potential market for or value of the copyrighted work.

When an infringement case is brought and the defendant claims the fair use defense, the court looks at the above factors, frequently giving the most weight to the fourth factor.

Red Flag Situations

1. *Situation:* A company buys one copy of a popular book on business ethics, makes twenty copies on a duplicating machine, and distributes the copies to employees.

   Potential Problem: If the company is sued by the book's author (or publisher) for copyright infringement and claims the fair use exception, a court will rule for the plaintiff. Reviewing the four factors described above, the court will look most closely at the effect upon the potential sales and rule against the defendant.

2. *Situation:* A company employee makes unauthorized copies of a software program used at work and gives them to friends for free.

   Potential Problem: In 1997 Congress implemented the No Electronic Theft Act that makes it a crime to exchange copies of copyrighted electronic material without authority. In addition, making electronic copies without authority of music, books, magazines and movies for personal use is also a crime under the Act. Sanctions include $250,000 in fines and up to five years in prison.

Going Global

1. Copyright laws vary throughout the world. If your company shows movies or plays music in its foreign operations, make certain all required fees are paid to avoid copyright infringement.

2. If you are a copyright holder, consult with an attorney familiar with international copyright laws to learn how to protect your copyright in other countries.

3. Copyright laws are not stringently enforced in some countries; it is therefore necessary for a copyright holder to monitor constantly for infringements abroad.

Reducing Your Risks

1. Review the materials available from the Motion Picture Licensing Corporation (MPLC) to determine if your business is involved in "public" showings of copyrighted material; if so, pay the required annual fee for an "umbrella license."

2. Review the materials available from ASCAP to determine if your business is involved in the playing of copyrighted music; if so and if your company does not fall into the

limited exceptions, make certain the required fee is paid annually.

3. If your business owns works that are copyrightable, copyright the works with the U. S. Copyright Office.

4. Frequently certain works of intellectual property hold both copyright and trademark protection, such as certain Disney characters. Make sure your business does not use copyrighted works in its operations (such as paintings on the wall) without permission.

Sources of Information

1. For information on what material can be protected by copyright and how to register a copyright visit the U. S. Copyright Office at *http://www.loc.gov/copyright*.

2. Recent U.S. Supreme Court decisions on copyrights and international copyright treaties are available at *http://www.law.cornell.edu/topics/copyright.html*.

3. Additional copyright information is available from the Cyberspace Law Institute at *http://www.cli.org*.

4. For information on umbrella licenses for videos, go to *http://www.mplc.com*.

5. For information on umbrella licenses for musical works, visit *http://www.ascap.com*.

6. Information related to international protection of your intellectual property rights is available at *http://www.lexmercatoria.net/*

7. Additional information on copyrights is available at *http://www.swlearning.com/blaw/fundamentals/fundamentals5e/fundamentals5e.html*. Go to "Internet Applications" and click on Chapter 5, "Intellectual Property and Internet Law."

Corporation

(For additional information on forms of business organization, *see **Limited Liability Corporations**; **Limited Liability Partnerships**; **Limited Partnerships; Partnerships;** and **Sole Proprietorships***.)

A ***corporation*** is a statutorily authorized form of business operation that is an entity separate and apart from its shareholders. State statutes govern the formation and operation of a corporation. A corporation is referred to as a statutory entity because its existence is based on statutory (written) laws authorizing its existing.

Classifications: A corporation that operates within the state of its incorporation is referred to as a domestic corporation. A corporation operating in a state other than the one where it was incorporated (i.e., a New York corporation operating in Virginia) is referred to as a foreign corporation. An alien corporation is one that was incorporated in another country and is doing business in the U.S. (For additional information on the various types of corporations, *see Close Corporations and S Corporations*.)

Advantages of the corporate form of business organization

1. *Limited Liability.* The major advantage is limited personal liability. As a general rule, an incorporator's liability is limited to the capital invested by the incorporator in the corporation. An exception is when a plaintiff in a lawsuit is allowed to "pierce the corporate veil" and recover from an owner's personal assets. The corporate veil may be pierced when: (a) the owner uses the corporation as an "alter ego" or (b) the corporation is undercapitalized, indicating there was no serious intent on the owner's part to establish a serious business.

Red Flag Situation

Situation: A restaurant owner takes a world cruise, charging the entire cost to the restaurant. The cruise was in no way connected to the business. The cruise line sues to collect the $10,000 owed and the restaurant owner refuses to pay, claiming the restaurant has only $100 in assets.

Potential Problem: The cruise line may be able to "pierce the corporate veil" because the restaurant owner was using the corporation as an alter ego. The restaurant owner is then personally liable for the debt.

2. *Perpetual existence.* Corporations continue in existence even when an incorporator dies or becomes incapacitated.

3. *Larger amount of available capital.* Due to the capital contributions of more than one owner, a corporation may find it easier to obtain loans than other forms of business entities.

4. *Combined expertise.* Different owners can bring different talents to the business.

5. *Workload delegation.* Corporate owners may either share the work or delegate to employees.

Disadvantages of the corporate form

1. *Fees for incorporation.* State law requires a corporation to pay a fee before receiving its corporate charter. In addition, accountant and attorney fees are frequently incurred in the process.

2. *Record keeping.* According to state corporation statutes, detailed record keep-

ing is required if a business is to receive the benefits afforded to a corporation. These records include minutes of directors' meetings and shareholder meetings.

3. *Required meetings.* State corporation laws require a minimum of one shareholder meeting per year with proper notice provided prior to the meeting.

Comparing the Corporation with Other Forms of Businesses

1. *Liability of Owners:*

a. Corporation: As mentioned, a major advantage of the corporation is limited personal liability of the owners (shareholders).

b. Limited Liability Company (LLC): The LLC form was first adopted in Wyoming in 1977. Today all the states have statutes authorizing this form. The LLC offers the corporation's advantage of limited personal liability for its owners. A recent Wyoming case held that the concept of "piercing the corporate veil" (see above) also applies to the LLC.

c. Partnership: A disadvantage of a general partnership is that the general partners face unlimited personal liability for the debts of the partnership.

d. Limited Partnership: A limited partnership is comprised of at least one general partner and an unlimited number of limited partners. The general partner faces unlimited personal liability while the limited partners are generally liable only to the extent of their investments.

e. Limited Liability Partnership (LLP): The LLP form is utilized by professionals. The LLP began in Texas in 1991 and today all states allow this form. An advantage of the LLP is that generally a partner is not personally liable for the negligence (malpractice) of the other partners. The degree of limitation varies among the states. Certain aspects of law regarding this form are unsettled at this time. For example, the question of whether the LLP form protects an innocent partner from personal liability outside of the state of formation is not clear.

f. Sole Proprietorship: The sole proprietor faces unlimited personal liability for the debts of the business.

2. *Tax Consequences*

a. Corporation: A frequently cited disadvantage of the corporate form is the "double taxation" factor. This refers to the fact that the corporation pays taxes on its profits and the shareholders pay taxes on their dividends.

b. LLC: An advantage of this hybrid form is that the owners can elect whether to pay taxes as a partnership or as a corporation. If they choose the partnership form, the partners pay the taxes (rather than the business paying) and the partners

61

deduct expenses on their personal tax forms.

    c. Partnership: A general partnership is not considered a separate tax-paying enti-
ty by the IRS. As a result, the partners show partnership profits and losses on
their tax returns.

    d. Limited Partnerships: The partners pay their pro rata share of taxes.

    e. LLP: Partners pay their pro rata share of taxes.

    f. Sole Proprietorship: The owner is taxed personally.

Uniform Laws of Corporations: As mentioned, a corporation is a statutory crea-
ture created by state statute. In order to assure more uniformity in corporation law,
most states have adopted either the Model Business Corporation Act (MBCA) or the
Revised Model Business Corporation Act (RMBCA).

Corporate Powers: According to the RMBCA, unless prohibited by its articles, a
corporation has "...the same powers as an individual to do all things necessary or con-
venient to carry out its business and affairs." (Sect. 3.02, RMBCA). The corporation is
expressly authorized to perform certain acts as set out in its articles, bylaws, and board
resolutions.

When a corporation engages in an act for which there is no authority, the act is
referred to as ultra vires ("beyond the powers"). In that situation, shareholders may sue
for an injunction or for damages. The officers and directors involved in the act can be
sued by the corporation. In addition, the state's attorney general can also sue.

Going Global

1. Laws governing the formation of a corporation vary greatly throughout the world.
   In some countries, a majority of the shareholders must be citizens of the country
   of incorporation. Failure to strictly adhere to corporate law can result in personal
   liability for the corporate owners.

2. A major decision for a domestic corporation going abroad is whether to set up a
   branch or a subsidiary. The tax consequences and potential vicarious liability for
   branches and subsidiaries vary greatly from one country to another.

Reducing Your Risks

1. Consult with an attorney and an accountant prior to determining what form of
   business organization to use because there are many legal and financial consequences. For example, a corporation pays tax on its income and shareholders also
   pay tax on dividends received. An individual corporate owner is not allowed to
   declare corporate expenses on the individual's own income tax statement.

2. Make certain no corporate assets are utilized for personal purposes so a plaintiff can "pierce the corporate veil" and recover your personal assets.

3. Review carefully the requirements for forming and maintaining a corporation in your state. Failure to strictly adhere to statutory requirements can result in losing the benefits of the corporate structure.

4. If you are considering forming a corporation in another country, seek accounting and legal advice from professionals familiar with the requirements in the host country prior to taking any action.

5. Seek competent advice as to whether to establish a branch or a subsidiary form of operation when your corporation goes abroad.

Sources of Information

1. Information on state corporation laws can be accessed through Cornell University at *http://www.law.cornell.edu/topics/state_statutes.html.*

2. Another source of information is through the University of Cincinnati College of Law at *http://www.law.uc.edu/CCL.*

3. Online information from individual states is also available from the Office of the Secretary of State.

4. For information on foreign corporation laws visit the World Trade Organization at *http://www.wto.org.*

5. Additional information is available at *http://www.swlearning.com/blaw/fundamentals/fundamentals6e/fundamentals6e.html.* Click on "Interactive Study Center" and go to Chapter 25, "Corporate Formation, Financing, and Termination."

Covenant Not to Compete

(For additional information, *see* the Legality section under ***Contract***.)

A ***covenant not to compete*** is basically an agreement where one party agrees not to compete with another party for a specified period of time within a certain geographic area. These covenants are frequently included in employment contracts and in contracts selling the goodwill of a business.

When Covenants Are Legal: As a general rule, any agreement that is in restraint of trade is considered against public policy and is therefore unenforceable. One exception to this rule involves certain covenants not to compete. As mentioned, they are frequently included in two types of contracts:

1. *Employment contracts:* Many employment contracts today include a provision where the employee agrees that, upon leaving the present employer, the worker will not compete for a certain period of time within a specific geographic area. Many states enforce these covenants provided they are reasonable as to the time element and the geographic area. In some states, if one or both elements of reasonableness are missing, the court will "reform" the contract, make it reasonable, and enforce it. Other states hold if either term is unreasonable the contract will not be reformed and is therefore unenforceable.

In a few states, a covenant not to compete contained within an employment contract is always illegal. Other states require the employer to provide a benefit to the employee in exchange for signing the covenant.

Red Flag Situation

Situation: A company includes in its employment contract for salespersons the provision that the worker will not compete for five years throughout the state. *Potential problem:* A court will probably rule these provisions are unreasonable. In some states, the court will "reform" and enforce the covenant. In other states, the contract will not be reformed.

2. *Selling the Goodwill of the Business:* A covenant not to compete is usually included in a contract to sell the goodwill of a business. A majority of states will enforce this covenant provided it is ancillary to a sales contract and meets the reasonableness tests. Due to the fact the buyer is paying additional money for the goodwill (the reputation of the business), courts usually allow longer time frames and broader geographic areas.

Red Flag Situation

Situation: An existing accounting firm is purchased for a large sum of money. The buyer does not include a covenant not to compete. *Potential problem:* The former owner of the firm can immediately set up a new firm within the same area and compete directly with the new owner.

Going Global

1. In some countries, all covenants not to compete are illegal. If you plan to include a covenant in an employment contract for your foreign workers, confirm that the covenant is enforceable.

2. When purchasing a business entity abroad, verify that you can legally include a covenant restricting the former owner from competing.

Sources of Information

1. To learn more about unenforceable contracts, go to *http://www.swlearning.com/blaw/fundamentals/fundamentals6e/fundamentals6e.html.* Click on "Interactive Study Center" and go to Chapter 9, "Capacity and Legality."

2. Information on employment law in Canada is available at *http://www.lawlib.utoronto.ca/resources/topic/employ.htm.*

Dd

Damages

The term *damages* refers to the monetary award a plaintiff receives in a civil lawsuit. Types of damages include *compensatory damages*, *consequential damages*, *punitive damages*, and *liquidated damages*. According to contract law, the plaintiff has the duty to mitigate (reduce) the damages suffered.

1. *Compensatory damages* are based on the amount of damages the plaintiff actually suffered. The purpose of compensatory damages is to place the injured party in the position the party would be in if the defendant had fully performed.

Assume a major manufacturer of electronics agreed to deliver 500 television sets priced at $300 per set to a retail store. The seller breached the contract and the buyer had to pay $320 per set elsewhere. In this case, the plaintiff buyer will receive $10,000 in compensatory damages based on the additional $20 per set required to purchase the sets elsewhere.

2. *Consequential damages* are damages that result or "flow from" the defendant's breach. Assume a tree nursery agreed to deliver 300 fir trees to a grocery store by December 10. The trees were delivered on December 26. The buyer can prove all trees would have sold at a profit of $20 per tree. In this case, the buyer can recover $6,000 in consequential damages for the lost profits that resulted from defendant's breach. In this situation, the seller knew (or should have known) the

67

trees could not be sold after Christmas Day. In order to recover consequential damages, the plaintiff must prove the defendant knew or should have known of the consequences that would flow from the breach.

Red Flag Situation

Situation: A printing shop orders a part for its printing press from a supplier who agrees to deliver the part the following day (June 5). The part is delivered on June 8. As a result of the delay in delivery, the printing shop could not fulfill its commitment to print an advertising flyer on time and therefore lost $2000 in profits it would have realized from the job. The supplier was unaware of the consequences of the late delivery.

Potential Problem: In order for a plaintiff to recover consequential damages, the plaintiff must prove the defendant knew or should have known of the consequence that would result from the breach. In this situation, the printing shop will probably not be able to recover for lost profits.

3. *Punitive damages* are sometimes referred to as "punishment damages." They are awarded either as a means of punishment for what the court considers outrageous behavior on the defendant's part or as a deterrent for future wrongdoers. Punitive damages are ordinarily not awarded in breach of contract cases.

4. *Liquidated damages* are agreed to by the parties in the event of a future dispute and are included within the contract.

Red Flag Situation

Situation: A corporation owns a commercial building. An accountant has a one-year lease for the tenth floor of the building at $15,000 per month. Six months after the contract begins, the tenant breaches the contract and vacates the building.

Potential Problem: According to contract law, the injured party must make a good faith attempt to mitigate the damages. As a result, building owner must try to rent the tenth floor to other tenants for the remaining six months of the contract. Assume the space is immediately rented to a new tenant for $14,000 per month. The plaintiff can then sue the accountant for compensatory damages of $6,000.

Going Global

1. Many countries do not award consequential damages. For that reason, a plaintiff may seek to have a case tried in the U. S. rather than abroad in order to claim these damages. For the same reason, a defendant in a case brought in the U.S. may try to have the case moved to a foreign court.

2. An increasing number of international contracts contain a "choice of forum"

clause whereby the parties agree in advance that if a dispute arises the case will be tried in the designated country. Contracts frequently also contain a "choice of law" clause providing what country's laws will apply in case a dispute arises.

Reducing Your Risks

1. Maintain records necessary to document your losses in case you must bring a lawsuit in the future.

2. Require a contract be in writing even if it is not covered by the Statute of Frauds.

3. Make certain the other party knows the consequences you will suffer in case of breach of contract so you may successfully claim consequential damages.

4. Prior to entering into an international contract, consult with a competent attorney regarding possible choice of forum and choice of law clauses in the contract.

Sources of Information

1. Additional information on damages is available at *http://www.law.cornell.edu/topics/contracts.html*.

2. To learn more, go to *http://www.swlearning.com/blaw/fundamentals/fundamentals6e/fundamentals6e.html*. Click on "Interactive Study Center" and go to Chapter 12, "Breach and Remedies."

Defamation

(For additional information, *see Disparagement of Property* and *Torts*.)

The term *defamation* refers to the intentional tort based on the defendant's false statement that is harmful to the plaintiff's reputation and is published to at least one other person. Written defamation is referred to as libel and spoken defamation is referred to as slander.

Requirements for defamation: The plaintiff in a defamation suit must prove the following three elements:

1. the statement made by defendant was false;

2. the statement is harmful to defendant's reputation; and

3. the statement was published to at least one other person.
   Dictating a letter to one's secretary meets the publication requirement. The publication requirement is also met if a third party overhears the defendant making the statement to plaintiff.

Defenses:

1. Truth is the ultimate defense in a defamation case.

2. Privilege refers to certain statements that, although defamatory, are protected. Protected statements include those made by attorneys in courtroom proceedings and statements made by members of the U.S. Congress during debate on the Congress floor.

3. Absence of malice applies when the plaintiff is a public figure. In this situation, the plaintiff must prove malice on the defendant's part in order to win. Malice means the defendant either: (a) knew the statement was false or (b) made the statement with reckless disregard for the truth.

Red Flag Situation

Situation: A supervisor accuses an employee of embezzling money from the company's cash box. The supervisor makes the accusation in the presence of another employee. The money later shows up, proving the employee did not embezzle.

Potential Problem: The employee may successfully sue for the intentional tort of defamation. The statement was false, it injured the employee's reputation, and it was "published." The supervisor's employer faces potential liability because an employer is liable for an employee's tort committed "within the scope of employment." (The supervisor also faces potential liability for the tort.)

Going Global

Agency law in many other countries recognizes the liability of the employer for an employee's tort committed "within the scope of employment." A U.S. based employer may therefore be liable for a defamatory statement made by an employee working in another country.

Reducing Your Risk

1. Make certain your employees understand the elements of defamation. An injurious statement in an employee evaluation or in a letter of recommendation for a former employee may prove to be defamatory.

2. Consult with competent counsel regarding your company's policy on handling employees suspected of wrongdoing. An accusation that turns out to be false (or one a court believes to be false) can lead to a lawsuit.

3. Make certain employees understand that statements made through e-mail and in chat rooms on the Internet can be defamatory.

Sources of Information

1. Additional information is available at *http://www.law.cornell.edu/topics/torts/html.*

2. To learn more, go to *http://www.swlearning.com/blaw/fundamentals/fundamentals6e/fundamentals6e.html.* Click on "Interactive Study Center" and go to Chapter 4, "Torts and Cyber Torts."

Delegation of Duty

(For additional information, *see Contract*.)

The term *delegation of duty* refers to a situation where a party to a contract (delegator) delegates a contractual duty of performance to a third party (delegatee).

Nondeligable Duties: In certain situations, a duty cannot be delegated:

1. When the contract prohibits delegation of duties.

2. When performance requires personal skills or talents.

3. When the contract involves the obligor's personal trust.

4. When a third party's performance will be materially different from the performance expected by the party to whom the duty is owed (the obligee).

Red Flag Situation

Situation: A hauling company agrees to pick up debris at a construction site and deliver it to the city landfill. The hauling company delegates its duty to a trash company and the latter does not perform.

Potential Problem: The obligor remains liable on a contract even if the duty of performance has been delegated to a third party. The construction company can sue the hauling company as the original obligor on the contract.

Going Global

Duties that cannot be delegated in one country may be delegable elsewhere. If a party wants assurance the obligor will not delegate the duty of performance, the contract should provide the duty is not delegable.

Reducing Your Risk

1. If you want to make sure the obligor does not delegate the duty of performance, include a non-delegation provision in the contract.

2. If your company decides to delegate its duty of performance to a third party, make certain that party is responsible. Delegation of duty does not relieve the original obligor of the duty to perform.

Sources of Information

1. Contract law information can be found at *http://www.law.cornell.edu/topics/contracts.html*.

2. For additional information, go to *http://www.swlearning.com/blaw/fundamentals/fundamentals6e/fundamentals6e.html*. Click on "Interactive Study Center" and go to Chapter 11, "Third Party Rights and Discharge."

Discrimination

(*See Employment Discrimination*.)

Disparagement of Property

(For additional information, *see Defamation* and *Torts*.)

The intentional business tort referred to as ***disparagement of property*** involves published false statements that harm the plaintiff economically.

Types of disparagement of property:

1. Slander of title refers to a published false statement that raises doubt regarding the plaintiff's legal ownership of property or claims plaintiff is not the legal owner.

2. Slander of quality refers to a published false statement regarding the plaintiff's product. This is sometimes referred to as trade libel.

In certain cases, a false statement may be considered both disparagement and defamation. For example, if a defendant falsely claims a local florist sells stolen flowers, the florist may sue for slander of title and for defamation (injury to personal reputation).

Red Flag Situation

Situation: A salesperson at a local jewelry store tells a customer that the jewelry being sold by a competing jeweler is counterfeit.

Potential Problem: If the statement is false, the competing jeweler may sue the local store for slander of quality. This is another example of a tort committed by an employee "within the scope of employment" and therefore the employer may be liable.

Going Global

Tort laws vary throughout the world. The tort of disparagement of property is considered a very serious offense in many countries.

Reducing Your Risk

1. Remember that a derogatory statement made about a competitor may lead to a lawsuit for disparagement of property if the plaintiff meets certain requirements.

2. Caution employees that statements made through e-mail and chat rooms may result in liability if the requirements for defamation or disparagement of property are met.

Sources of Information

1. For more information on e-mail and chat rooms, refer to the Cyberspace Law Institute at *http://www.cli.org*.

2. To learn more about defamation and disparagement of property, visit *http://www.swlearning.com/blaw/fundamentals/fundamentals6e/fundamentals6e.html*. Click on "Interactive Study Center" and go to Chapter 4, "Torts and Cyber Torts."

Duress

(For additional information, *see* the Genuine Assent section of ***Contract.***)

According to contract law, ***duress*** occurs when a party enters into a contract due to threats of harm by the other contracting party. The contract is voidable on the victim's part. Therefore, the victim has the power to either enforce or avoid the contract.

Ee

E-Contracts

(For additional information, *see Contracts*.)

A contract entered into by utilizing some form of electronic commerce is referred to as an *e-contract*. Examples include contracts entered into via e-mail, fax, and over the Internet. Billions of dollars are involved in e-contracts globally on an annual basis. As a general rule, the basic rules of contract law apply to e-contracts in the U.S. Special problem areas relative to e-contracts include signatures, click-on agreements, electronic agents and shrink-wrap agreements:

Electronic signatures (e-signatures): State laws relative to e-signatures are not consistent. In 1999, the National Conference of Commissioners on Uniform State Laws adopted the Uniform Electronic Transactions Act (UETA). The UETA has been presented to the various states for adoption. Today over 40 states have adopted all or part of the Act. The UETA will apply if both parties agree to contract via e-commerce. According to the UETA, an otherwise valid signature will not become invalid because it is in electronic form.

The federal Electronic Signatures in Global and National Commerce Act (E-SIGN Act) became law in 2000. According to this act, an otherwise valid sigture will not become invalid because it is in electronic form. The E-SIGN Act also requires: (1) the parties agree in advance to the use of electronic signatures and (2) the document can be reproduced and retained. The Act does not apply to certain transactions including foreclosures, health-insurance terminations, divorce decrees and wills.

Click-On Agreements: An agreement whereby an offeree agrees to the terms of an offer by pressing a button indicating agreement is referred to as a ***click-on agreement***. As a general rule, a click-on agreement is considered a valid acceptance.

Red Flag Situation

Situation: An accountant in a large firm decides to use a new accounting software program at work. In a hurry, the accountant scrolls through all of the information relative to warranties and restrictions on use without reading the terms. The accountant immediately goes to the end of the agreement and "clicks on" the acceptance button. Six months later the accountant discovers a defect in the program and tries to return it. The software company points out the contract provided only a 90-day warranty.

Potential Problem: By clicking on the acceptance button, the accountant agreed to all of the terms in the agreement. Failure to read the terms is no excuse.

Electronic Agent: An electronic agent, or e-agent, is basically a computer program that represents the principal in an on-line search or on-line transaction. (For additional information, see Agency.) According to agency law, the principal is liable for a contract entered into by an agent if the agent had some form of authority.

Shrink-wrap Agreement: When a buyer purchases computer software (and other forms of goods) and the purchase agreement is enclosed in the plastic wrap encompassing the goods, the agreement is referred to as a shrink-wrap agreement. The agreement is usually between the manufacturer and the purchaser rather than between the purchaser and the retailer. As a general rule, the courts have held that a shrink-wrap agreement is valid provided it meets the usual requirements for a valid contract. The courts do not consistently uphold shrink-wrap agreements, however. Assume the buyer is a consumer (not a merchant), enters into a contract to purchase shrink-wrap goods, and then learns of additional terms in the shrink-wrap later. Some courts will not enforce the additional terms if the buyer objects to the terms.

Going Global

1. Laws in the European Union, Japan and China provide for the validity of e-signatures when certain requirements are met.

2. The United Nations Commission on International Trade Law (UNCITRAL) Model Law on Electronic Commerce provides for the legal recognition of electronic signatures.

Reducing Your Risks

1. Understand that failure to read the provisions of a click-on agreement is no defense when the seller holds you to the terms of the agreement.

2. Remember that failure to read the terms of a shrink-wrap agreement may not be considered a valid defense when the manufacturer claims you have violated the agreement.

3. Exercise care in utilizing an e-agent to represent you or your company online. Courts generally hold that the principal may be liable for actions of the e-agent even when the principal was unaware of the action.

Sources of Information

1. To view information about the National Conference of Commissioners on Uniform State Laws, visit *http://www.nccusl.org*. This site also provides a list of states that have adopted the Uniform Computer Information Transactions Act (UCITA) and the Uniform Electronic Transactions Act (UETA).

2. UNCITRAL provisions on electronic contracts are available at *http://www. uncitral.org*.

3. More information is available at *http://www.swlearning.com/blaw/ fundamentals/fundamentals6e/fundamentals6e.html*. Click on "Interactive Study Center" and go to Chapter 13, "E Contracts."

E-Mail

(For additional information, *see E-Contracts*.)

The term *e-mail* refers to mail that is transmitted electronically. Methods of electronic transmission include the Internet and telephones. Two aspects of e-mail are of particular concern in today's workplace: the privacy issue and an employer's potential liability.

Privacy and E-mail: Millions of e-mail messages are exchanged daily in the workplace. Many of the messages sent and received by employees are personal in nature and not work-related. Concerned over potential employer liability for the contents of these messages, an increasing number of employers are monitoring the e-mails transmitted at work. In response, some employees have claimed this practice is a violation of privacy.

Red Flag Situation

Situation: A male supervisor at a national manufacturing company sends private e-mails at work to three female employees. The messages contain jokes that are derogatory of the employees' sex. The three females sue the manufacturing company claiming sexual harassment in the workplace.

Potential Problem: Despite the fact the messages were sent via private e-mail and the company was not aware of them, a court may hold the employer is liable for the sexual harassment at the workplace. Courts are trying to balance the right to privacy (through an e-mail) vis-à-vis an employee's right to work in an environment free of harassment. In many jurisdictions, the employer has the right to monitor an employee's e-mail provided certain requirements are met. The employer should consult with an attorney familiar with employment law in the employer's jurisdiction relative to appropriate steps to take.

Employer's Potential Liability: As the example above illustrates, an employer may be liable for e-mails which discriminate or cause a hostile environment in the workplace. In addition, an employer may be liable for defamatory remarks made by an employee "within the scope of employment." (For additional information on employer liability, *see Agency*.)

Red Flag Situation

Situation: An employee of a major retail chain sends an e-mail to a company employee in another city stating that a competing retailer is selling "knock-off" purses and advertising them as designer items. The statement is false. The competitor learns of the e-mail and sues the major retail chain for the employee's defamatory statements. (For additional information, *see Defamation*.)

Potential Problem: An employer is liable for the torts of the employee committed "within the scope of employment." In this situation, the employer may be liable for the defamatory e-mail.

Going Global

1. Laws relevant to privacy vary among the countries. If your company operates abroad, consult with an attorney familiar with the laws of the host country if you are considering monitoring the e-mail of your employees in the foreign office.

2. Tort laws in many countries recognize the vicarious liability of an employer for the torts committed by an employee "within the scope of employment." Become familiar with the tort laws in the host country to determine if you may be liable for any defamatory statements made by an employee via e-mail. Although a statement may not be defamatory in the country of the sender, it may be considered defamatory

in the country of the recipient. In that case, the employer may face liability.

3. Chat rooms are frequently the sites of potentially defamatory statements. A court may determine that a statement made through a chat room is a tort in one of the countries where the statement is read; the employer may then face potential liability.

4. The law is not settled on how and when professionals (i.e., accountants and attorneys) can communicate with clients via e-mail without violating the requirement for professional/client confidentiality. Professionals subject to confidentially requirements should become familiar with the requirements within the applicable jurisdiction.

Reducing Your Risks

1. Obtain legal advice relevant to the legal issues involved in monitoring the e-mail of your employees. Make certain you comply with all requirements relevant to monitoring.

2. Make certain employees understand that statements made through e-mail (including Chat Rooms) can be defamatory.

3. Understand that the tort of invasion of privacy can occur through e-mail (for additional information, see Torts). A statement made about another party may be true but may still lead to liability for invasion of privacy.

4. The laws regarding e-mail are changing on a regular basis. It is important to monitor these changes.

Sources of Information

1. Information on employment issues is available at *http://www.aflcio.org*.

2. Employment discrimination issues are addressed at *http://www.eeoc.gov*.

3. To learn more, go to *http://www.swlearning.com/blaw/fundamentals/fundamentals6e/fundamentals6e.html*. Click on "Interactive Study Center" and go to Chapter 23, "Employment Law."

Eminent Domain

The legal theory that allows a sovereign government to take privately owned real property for a public purpose is referred to as ***eminent domain***. The Fifth Amendment of the U.S. Constitution provides "...nor shall private property be taken for public use, without just compensation." The U.S. Constitution therefore provides that two requirements must be met in order for a governmental entity to exercise its right of eminent domain: (1) the taking of the property must be for a public purpose and (2) the owner must be fairly compensated for the taking. The property owner has the right to appeal if the taking (also referred to as the condemnation) is not for a public purpose or the owner believes the compensation is unfair. In recent years the definition of "public purpose" has been expanded in the U.S.

The U.S. Supreme Court recently upheld a city's right to exercise the right of eminent domain and take private property for development purposes. In *Kelo, et.al. v. City of New London* (125 S. Ct. 2655), the Court held that the city's proposed sale of plaintiff's property for development purposes "qualifies as a 'public use' within the meaning of the Takings Clause." (Decided June 23, 2005).

Red Flag Situation

Situation: A financial planning firm is considering the purchase of a tract of land in the city limits for its new office site. The purchaser does not meet with the city planning and zoning office to determine if the city has future plans to utilize the land for a public purpose. The firm buys the land and constructs a large office building.

Potential Problem: The city has long-range plans to condemn (take) certain tracts of land and convert them to parks. The site of the office building is one of those tracts that is condemned.

Going Global

A major political risk for companies investing in real property abroad involves the taking of private property by the foreign government. A taking that provides no payment to the property owner is referred to as confiscation.

Reducing Your Risks

1. Prior to the purchase of any real property, check with local, state and federal offices that may have information relevant to long-term plans for the taking of the property for public purposes. For example, the state transportation department may plan to construct a new highway through the middle of the land.

2. If your company receives a condemnation notice, confirm that the taking of the property is for a public purpose and that the amount offered is a fair amount. If either of these conditions is not met, you can appeal. Relevant to the amount offered, seek expert advice relevant to the value of the property.

Sources of Information

1. To learn more about property law, go to *http://www.law.cornell.edu.* Click on "Property, Natural Resources, the Environment."

2. Political risk assessment is discussed at *http://www.opic.gov.*

3. More information is available at *http://www.swlearning.com/blaw/ fundamentals/fundamentals6e/fundamentals6e.html.* Click on "Interactive Study Center" and go to Chapter 29, "Real Property."

Employee Retirement Income Security Act

The *Employee Retirement Income Security Act (ERISA)* is a federal law that establishes certain standards for those businesses that choose to have private pension plans for their employees. The U.S. Department of Labor is responsible for enforcing the law through its Labor Management Services Administration.

Red Flag Situation

Situation: A new company decides to establish a private pension fund for its employees. The parties responsible for establishing and maintaining the fund do not review the ERISA requirements for the fund.

Potential Problem: Failure to comply with the ERISA requirements relevant to maintaining the fund can lead to civil and criminal sanctions.

Going Global

1. Labor laws vary greatly throughout the world. If you purchase an operating business in another country, you may be bound by the existing labor union contract between the former owner and the union. That union contract may include specific provisions for employee retirement funds.

2. If your business controls an overseas operation that employs U.S. citizens and your company has a private pension fund for employees in this country, confirm what your obligations are relevant to the overseas employees.

Reducing Your Risks

1. As a result of recent corporate scandals, U.S. laws relevant to employee pension funds are changing. Review the latest laws as they apply to your business.

2. Understand that mishandling of pension funds can lead to both criminal and civil sanctions. Lawsuits may be filed by the federal government and also by employees.

Sources of Information

1. To learn more about ERISA, visit the U. S. Department of Labor site at *http://www.dol.gov.*

2. Additional information on labor issues is available at *http://www.aflcio.org.*

3. To learn more, go to *http://www.swlearning.com/blaw/fundamentals/fundamentals6e/fundamentals6e.html.* Click on "Interactive Study Center" and go to Chapter 23, "Employment Law."

Employment Discrimination

(*See Age Discrimination; Americans with Disabilities Act; Civil Rights Act of 1964; Family and Medical Leave Act; Occupational Safety and Health Act;* and *Pregnancy Discrimination Act of 1978.*)

Equal Employment Opportunity Commission

(For additional information, *see Civil Rights Act of 1964.*)

The *Equal Employment Opportunity Commission (EEOC)* is the federal agency responsible for enforcing Title VII of the Civil Rights Act of 1964. Prior to filing a lawsuit based on a Title VII claim, the aggrieved employee must first file a complaint and seek a ruling from the EEOC.

Red Flag Situation

Situation: A manufacturing company sells its product throughout the U.S. and employs 150 employees. The company has not appointed an Equal Employment Officer and has no information available to employees regarding the rights regarding employment discrimination.

Potential Problem: Among those businesses subject to Title VII of the Civil Rights Act are businesses engaged in interstate commerce that employ at least 15 workers. Title VII has specific requirements regarding the appointment of an equal employment officer and the posting of information regarding employment discrimination. Failure to comply can lead to lawsuits by the federal government and also by employees.

Going Global

Title VII of the Civil Rights Act applies to U.S. citizens working abroad for an employer that is under the control of a U.S. company.

Reducing Your Risks

1. Determine if your domestic or foreign business is covered by Title VII of the Civil Rights Act of 1964. If so, make certain you are in compliance with EEOC regulations including the appointment of an equal employment officer and the posting of information regarding employee discrimination.

2. The EEOC issues new regulations on a continuing basis. Monitor these closely to assure compliance with the latest requirements.

3. Companies not subject to Title VII are still subject to state employment discrimination laws. Be familiar with these laws also.

Sources of Information

1. To learn more about the EEOC, visit *http://www.eeoc.gov*.

2. Additional information on employment discrimination is available at *http://www.dol.gov*.

3. More information is available at *http://www.swlearning.com/blaw/ fundamentals/fundamentals6e/fundamentals6e.html*. Click on "Interactive Study Center" and go to Chapter 23, "Employment Law."

Express Warranties

Express warranties are warranties expressly created by the seller or lessor pertaining to the real or personal property or to the services being offered for sale or lease. According to Article 2 of the Uniform Commercial Code (which covers the sale or lease of goods), an express warranty for goods may be created in three ways:

1. By making a factual assertion or promise about the goods or services.

2. Through the use of a descriptive word or phrase, such as "shatter-proof" or "rust-proof."

3. By providing a sample of the goods. Express warranties may be verbal or written.

The courts sometimes have to determine whether a statement by a seller or lessor was "sales talk" or "puffing" or created an express warranty. Assume a car dealer tells a prospective customer, "buy this car and you'll never regret it." The customer buys the car, immediately dislikes it, and sues for breach of express warranty. A court will probably determine the salesperson's statement was "puffing" and did not create an express warranty.

Red Flag Situation

Situation: A used car salesperson assures a customer that a car will get a minimum of 20 miles per gallon. Relying on the statement, the customer buys the car and then discovers it will only get 10 miles per gallon.

Potential Problem: The customer may sue for breach of an express warranty. The statement regarding mileage was a factual assertion, which created an express warranty.

Going Global

1. Laws regarding warranties vary throughout the world. If you are providing goods or services in another country, become familiar with contract law in the host country. Understand how an express warranty is created.

2. Many countries are signatories to the Convention for the International Sale of Goods (CISG). If you are selling goods to a merchant buyer whose place of business is in a signatory country, review the CISG provisions on warranties. (The parties may choose to "opt out" of the CISG.)

3. Many countries do not require a writing for a contract to be enforceable. To make certain both parties understand what warranties are included in the contract, a writing is still advisable.

Reducing Your Risks

1. Understand how an express warranty is created domestically and abroad. A salesperson or lessor may inadvertently create an express warranty by becoming overly enthusiastic in a sales pitch.

2. Review any labels or advertisements relevant to your goods or services. For example, a statement on a restaurant menu that all food is "Free of MSG" creates an express warranty.

Sources of Information

1. For more information on the CISG, visit *http://cisg.law.pace.edu/cisg/text/treaty.html.*

2. Learn more about contract law at *http://www.law.cornell.edu/topics.*

3. Information about the UCC in your state can be accessed by going to

http://www.law.cornell.edu and selecting your state and then "Commercial Law."

4. Additional information is available at *http://www.swlearning.com/blaw/funda-mentals/fundamentals6e/fundamentals6e.html.* Click on "Interactive Study Center" and go to Chapter 17, "Warranties and Product Liability."

Fair Debt Collection Practices Act

The federal *Fair Debt Collection Practices Act* (15 U.S.C. § 1691 ff), an amendment to the Consumer Credit Protection Act, regulates the activities of collection agencies in their attempts to collect for their clients. The law also applies to creditors collecting their own debts that use a third party's name in the process. Prohibited activities include contacting the debtor after a certain hour of the evening; contacting the debtor at work if the employer objects; engaging in harassing or intimidating methods; contacting the debtor (except in limited situations) after being informed the debtor will not pay; and notifying third parties of the debt (with limited exceptions).

In addition to the FDCPA (which regulates collection agencies), state laws regulate the collection procedures of creditors. In many states, these laws are very similar to the FDCPA.

Red Flag Situation

Situation: A local collection agency begins calling a debtor at midnight and harassing the debtor over the telephone.

Potential Problem: The debtor can sue the agency based on the Fair Debt Collection Practices Act that prohibits contacting the debtor late at night and engaging in harassment.

Going Global

Collection laws vary throughout the world. If your company is involved in debt collection abroad (either as the collection agency or a creditor collecting its own debt), be familiar with the collection laws in each country where you will be involved in the collection process. Violations carry heavy penalties in some parts of the world.

Reducing Your Risks

1. If you operate a collection agency, become familiar with the provisions of any debt collection practices laws (both state and federal) that regulate the debt collection process.

2. If your company engages in its own collection, understand the law that regulates your collection process.

3. Make certain your employees understand and adhere to laws applicable to the collection process.

Sources of Information

1. Additional information on debt collection is available at *http://www.law. cornell.edu/topics/consumer_credit.html.*

2. For information on laws in your state, go to the above site and click on "State Statutes."

3. Additional information is available at *http://www.swlearning.com/blaw/ fundamentals/fundamentals6e/fundamentals6e.html.* Click on "Interactive Study Center" and go to "Court Case Updates" and click on "Consumer Protection."

Fair Labor Standards Act

The federal *Fair Labor Standards Act (FLSA)* (29 U.S.C. §§ 201-219) became law in 1938. The law regulates child labor practices, minimum wages for certain workers, and overtime pay. In those states that also have their own overtime and minimum wage provisions, the employer must meet the provisions that are higher (state or federal). The FSLA also imposes certain record-keeping requirements on employers.

Employment of Children (Child Labor): The FLSA limits the types of jobs children under 14 may perform. Delivery of newspapers is an example of an allowable job. Children under 16 cannot work during school hours nor can they perform nonagricultural work for more than 18 hours during a school week. A work permit is required for children under 16 in many states. Hazardous activities are prohibited for anyone under 18. For a complete discussion on child labor restrictions, go to the U.S. Department of Labor's Web site at *http://www.dol.gov.*

Red Flag Situation

Situation: The owner of an accounting firm has a 15-year-old working in the office for 22 hours per week during the school year.

Potential Problem: The FLSA prohibits children under 16 working more than 18 hours during a school week.

Minimum Wage Provisions: At present, the minimum wage for nonexempt workers is $5.15 per hour. The rate is periodically raised by Congress.

Overtime Pay: According to the FLSA, nonexempt employees are entitled to a minimum overtime pay of one and one-half times their regular pay for work performed in excess of 40 hours per week. Overtime pay does not apply to working on weekends or holidays unless the 40 hours are exceeded. A "workweek" is comprised of seven consecutive 24-hour periods (168 hours total).

New regulations applicable to overtime pay became effective on August 23, 2004. The changes include the following provisions:

1. Employees in nonexempt categories who earn up to $455 per week ($23,660 annually) may qualify for overtime pay. (The previous limit was $250 per week.)

2. Employees earning over $100,000 are exempt from overtime pay.

3. Workers in positions classified as executive, professional or administrative or outside salesperson are exempt from overtime pay.

4. Workers classified as managers are exempt from overtime pay.

5. Certain computer workers are exempt.

According to the U.S. Department of Labor, the exemption from overtime pay applies when the worker's salary and specific duties meet the regulatory requirements.

Going Global

Labor laws vary throughout the world and businesses employing workers for overseas operations need to be familiar with the labor laws of the host country.

Reducing Your Risks

1. Remember that a business is subject to both federal and state labor laws. Become familiar with applicable laws in each state in which your company employs workers.

2. Prior to retaining workers overseas, review applicable labor laws.

3. Frequently a labor practice that is illegal at home is legal in the host country. Companies that engage in unfair (but legal) treatment of workers abroad are increasingly becoming the subject of adverse media attention in their home country. As a result, overall company revenue suffers.

Sources of Information

1. For information on current labor laws in the U.S., including the recent changes regarding overtime pay, visit the Department of Labor at *http://www.dol.gov*.

2. Information on international labor laws is available from the International Labor Organization at *http://www.ilo.org*.

3. For more information, go to *http://www.swlearning.com/blaw/fundamentals/ fundamentals6e/fundamentals6e.html.* Click on "Interactive Study Center" and click on "Court Case Updates" and go to "Employment Law."

False Imprisonment

(For additional information, *see Torts*)

The intentional tort of *false imprisonment* occurs when the defendant deprives the plaintiff of the right of freedom of movement without just cause. A business may face a false imprisonment claim by a plaintiff who was detained for suspected shoplifting. Although the suspect was not actually handcuffed, freedom of movement was hampered due to the fact the defendant could call the police if the suspect fled the scene.

At one time, businesses were regularly liable for false imprisonment if the suspect could convince a court no shoplifting occurred. Today, most states have statutes that protect the business from liability if certain requirements are met. These statutes (sometimes referred to as shopkeepers' privileges) provide the business is not liable for detaining a suspected shoplifter (who did not shoplift) provided the following requirements are met:

1. The business had probable cause to believe the suspect had engaged in shoplifting.

2. The detention was in a reasonable manner.

3. The detention was for a reasonable period of time.

These considerations involve factual determinations and it is up to a jury to make the factual determinations in a case. Juries have recently awarded large sums of money to plaintiffs in these cases.

Red Flag Situation

Situation: A salesperson in a retail store suspects a customer of shoplifting a shirt. The salesperson locks the suspect in an office for two hours without allowing the customer to show the receipt from another store for the shirt.

Potential problem: The store faces liability for false imprisonment. The plaintiff can successfully argue there was no probable cause because the plaintiff had a receipt for the shirt but was not allowed to show it. In addition, locking the defendant in an office for two hours was unreasonable as to the manner of detention and the time period.

Going Global

Laws on false imprisonment vary in other countries. If you are operating a business abroad where shoplifting is a problem, be familiar with the host country's laws on detention of suspected shoplifters.

Reducing Your Risks

1. Make certain only trained employees (or professional security staff) detain suspected shoplifters. Jury awards in the U.S. for false imprisonment claims have been extremely high in recent years.

2. Frequently a plaintiff claiming false imprisonment also claims **defamation**.

3. Falsely accusing a customer of shoplifting can meet the requirements for defamation and result in another high award.

4. Seek professional advice relative to the detention of suspected shoplifters including advice on where the detention should occur and in what manner. A recent court decision in your jurisdiction may impact your own procedures.

Sources of Information

1. Additional information on torts is available at *http://www.law.cornell.edu topics/torts/html.*

2. More tort information is available at *http://www.swlearning.com/blaw/fundamentals/fundamentals6e/fundamentals6e.html.* Go to "Court Case Updates" and click on "Torts."

Family and Medical Leave Act

(For additional information, see *Employment Discrimination*.)

The federal *Family and Medical Leave Act (FMLA)* (29 U.S.C. §§ 2601, 2611-2619, 2651-2654) became law in 1993. The law applies to businesses engaged in interstate commerce that employ at least 50 workers. The FMLA requires employers to allow nonexempt employees up to 12 weeks of unpaid leave for family and medical purposes every 12 months. The employer is generally required to continue the employee's health care insurance during the time off and provide employment in the same or a comparable position upon return to work. An employee must have worked for at least one year for the business and worked at least 1250 hours during the past year. Exempt from these provisions are employees who receive the top 10 per cent of pay in the company ("key employees").

In addition to the federal FMLA, employers are subject to state laws providing for family and medical leave.

Red Flag Situation

Situation: An employee who has worked fulltime for five years for a company requests two months of unpaid leave to care for an ill spouse. The employee is in the middle pay scale within the company. The employer denies the request. *Potential problem:* The employer may be sued for violation of the FMLA.

Going Global

1. Employment laws vary throughout the world. Many countries have laws mandating employers provide workers with leave for family and medical purposes.

2. If you purchase a business abroad, you may be subject to the provisions of the existing union contract; theses provisions may include a policy regarding family and medical leave for employees.

Reducing Your Risks

1. Review carefully all employee requests for family and medical leave in view of the FMLA requirements.

2. Make certain that employees returning from family or medical leave are provided with the same or comparable position they had before taking the leave.

3. Remember that your business is also subject to state laws addressing family and medical leave.

Sources of Information

1. The Department of Labor provides information at *http://www.dol/gov/esa/whd/fmla.*

2. Information on international labor laws is available at *http://www.ilo.org.*

3. For more information, go to*http://www.swlearning.com/blaw/fundamentals/fundamentals6e/fundamentals6e.html.* Click on "Court Case Updates" and go to "Employment Law."

Federal Trade Commission

In 1914, the *Federal Trade Commission (FTC)* was established as part of the Federal Trade Commission Act (15 U.S.C. §§ 45-48). The FTC is authorized to pass rules regulating trade practices, to conducting investigations, and to adjudicate certain trade disputes. In order to regulate trade practices, the FTC established the Bureau of Consumer Protection, the Bureau of Competition, and the Bureau of Economics.

Among its responsibilities, the FTC enforces regulations relevant to consumer rights, unfair trade practices, and illegal monopolies.

Major Areas of FTC Regulation

1. *Deceptive Advertising:* According to the FTC, an ad is deceptive if it will likely mislead a consumer. A statement that contains a misleading factual assertion is deceptive. If a celebrity advertises a product but does not use the product, the ad is considered deceptive.

Red Flag Situation

Situation: A major soft drink company runs an ad depicting a sports celebrity holding a can of the company's drink. In fact, the celebrity never drinks the product. The ad can be considered deceptive. The FTC may issue a cease and desist order to stop the ad and require counter ads to correct the misleading ad.

2. *Bait and Switch:* The FTC forbids running ads for a low-price product in order to "bait" the customer into the business and then "switch" to a higher priced item.

3. *Telemarketing Ads:* Based on the Telemarketing and Consumer Fraud and Abuse Prevention Act of 1994 (15 U.S.C. §§ 6101-6108), the FTC established its Telemarketing Sales Rules (16 C.F.R. §§ 310.1-310.8) The rules require telemarketers to tell the listeners the call is for sales purposes and to identify the seller and specify the item being sold.

4. *Additional Sales Regulations:* The FTC also regulates door-to-door sales, online sales, telephone sales, and mail-order sales.

5. *Monopolies:* The FTC is authorized to enforce the *Clayton Act* that prohibits illegal monopolistic and anticompetitive acts. Illegal practices include price discrimination, certain tying arrangements, and exclusive dealing contracts. The Act also prohibits mergers that adversely affect competition. Interlocking directorates are also prohibited when the undivided profits or capital surplus of either company exceeds an amount set by the FTC.

Going Global

1. Laws regarding deceptive advertising vary greatly throughout the world. Before launching an ad abroad, confirm that it does not violate the host country's advertising laws.

2. Laws relevant to monopoly power are more stringent in certain parts of the world. If you are considering a merger within the European Union, for instance, confirm that the merger meets the requirements of the EU Directive on mergers.

Reducing Your Risks

1. Both federal and state laws address deceptive advertising. Make certain your ads do not violate FTC or state regulations.

2. If you use a celebrity to endorse your product, confirm that the celebrity actually uses the product.

3. The FTC regulations are subject to change. Make certain you are familiar with the current regulations.

4. If your company is involved in telemarketing, become familiar with the Telephone Consumer Protection Act. The Act requires the caller to provide the name and telephone number or address of the party selling the goods or services.

Sources of Information

1. To learn more about the FTC and its role in regulating trade, visit *http://www.ftc.gov*.

2. More information on the Telephone Consumer Protection Act and the National Do Not Call Registry is available from the Federal Communications Commission at *http://www.fcc.gov*.

3. Additional information is available at *http://www.swlearning.com/blaw/fundamentals/fundamentals6e/fundamentals6e.html*. Click on "Court Case Updates" and go to "Consumer Protection."

Financing Statement

(For additional information, *see Secured Transactions.*)

According to the Uniform Commercial Code (UCC), a *financing statement* is a document "...normally filed to give pubic notice to third parties of the secured party's security interest." (UCC 9-102(a)(39)). The document is signed by a debtor granting the creditor security rights in certain collateral and is filed in the proper state office in order to place the world "on notice" of the security interest. The financing statement is particularly important when the same asset has been used as collateral for more than one debt. As a general rule, the first creditor to file a financing statement takes priority over later creditors. (There are exceptions to this rule that are discussed in *Secured Transactions.*) State law determines the proper place for filing.

Two steps are involved in a secured transaction: (1) attachment, whereby the security interest is created and (2) perfection, whereby the creditor gives notice of the interest. Filing of the financing statement is one means of perfection. (Attachment and perfection are discussed in detail in *Secured Transactions.*)

Perfection of the security interest is particularly important when the debtor pledges the same collateral for more than one debt. Perfection can occur by (1) filing the financing statement; (2) automatic perfection in certain types of transactions; and (3) the creditor retaining possession of the collateral until the debt is fully paid. (In today's business environment, the last approach is totally impractical.)

The form for the financing statement is establishing by the UCC (Section 9-521). Filing is according to the debtor's name.

Red Flag Situations

1. *Situation:* A computer company sells expensive computer equipment on credit to a financial planning firm. The seller does not require the buyer to sign a financing statement. The same computer equipment is used as collateral for a loan the firm receives later from the local bank. The bank requires the debtor to execute a security agreement and a financial statement. The latter is filed with the proper state office. The firm defaults on both debts.
   Potential Problem: By filing the financial statement, the bank perfected its security interest in the computer equipment and takes a priority interest in the collateral over the computer company (which failed to file a financing statement).

2. *Situation:* A bank loans money to a car dealer to purchase inventory. The lender files the signed financing statement. The statement only lists the inventory purchased (the autos) as the collateral.
   Potential problem: When the car dealer sells an auto to a customer in the ordi-

nary course of business, the customer has better rights to the car than the lender (despite the filing of the financial statement.) If the car dealer defaults on the loan, the bank cannot repossess the auto sold to the customer. The lender should have made certain the collateral listed on the financing statement included "proceeds" from the sale of the inventory.

Going Global

Laws on secured transactions vary greatly throughout the world. The methods for creating and perfecting the security interests also vary. If your company sells goods on credit or lends money abroad, become familiar with the host country's requirements for protecting your rights in the collateral.

Reducing Your Risks

1. If you are engaged in selling goods on credit or lending money, understand the requirements for assuring you will have priority in the collateral in case the debtor defaults.

2. Become familiar with the proper steps involved in repossessing collateral upon a debtor's default. (*See Secured Transactions.*) Violation of the proper repossession procedure can result in a lawsuit by the debtor.

3. Make certain employees understand the proper form required for the financing statement and confirm that the statement is filed in a timely manner.

Sources of Information

1. For more information on secured transactions, visit *http://www.law.cornell.edu/topics/secured_transactions.html.*

2. Additional information on filing financial statements is available at *http://www.swlearning.com/blaw/fundamentals/fundamentals6e/fundamentals6e.html.* Go to "Interactive Study Center" and click on Chapter 20, "Secured Transactions."

Foreign Corrupt Practices Act

(For additional information, *see Bribery*.)

The federal *Foreign Corrupt Practices Act (FCPA)* (15 U.S.C. §§ 78dd-1 ff) makes it illegal for U.S. businesspersons to offer a bribe to a foreign official or a candidate for office in order to obtain advantages for the defendant's business. Penalties for violation of the FCPA include fines and imprisonment. According to the Act, the crime is committed when the bribe is offered, even if the other party declines the offer. A 1998 amendment to the FCPA provides foreign individuals and companies are subject to the Act under certain circumstance.

In addition to the anti-bribery provisions, the FCPA also imposes certain record-keeping and accounting requirements on U.S. investors. Businesses must be able to detect a bribe of any amount.

Red Flag Situation

Situation: An overseas agent for a U.S. manufacturer is attempting to make a large sale to a foreign government. The agent offers the foreign official in charge of purchasing a family vacation in the U.S. if the U.S. company is awarded the contract.
Potential problem: The agent has violated the Foreign Corrupt Practices Act and the agent and the U.S. company face criminal sanctions.

Going Global

In the past, bribery of foreign officials was not considered a crime in many countries. (Some countries even permitted a business to deduct the bribery payment as a legitimate business expense.) Today, a number of the industrialized countries are signatories to a treaty that makes such bribery a crime.

Reducing Your Risks

1. Become familiar with the provisions of the Foreign Corrupt Practices Act.

2. Make certain your employees who are involved in negotiating contracts with foreign officials understand the Act and the serious consequences for violation.

3. If your company is contracting with foreign officials, become familiar with the bribery laws of the host country. In some parts of the world, bribery carries the death penalty.

4. If you are investing abroad, confirm that all employees responsible for record keeping and accounting understand the implications of the Act on their work.

Sources of Information

1. The U.S. Department of Justice provides information at *http://www.usdoj.gov/ criminal/fraud/fcpa.html.* Specific information on the FCPA is available through "The Lay-Person's Guide to the FCPA Statute" at this site.

2. Additional information is available at *http://www.swlearning.com/blaw/fundamentals/fundamentals6e/fundamentals6e.html.* Go to "Court Case Updates" and click on "Criminal Law" and "International Law."

Fraud

(For more information, *see Torts*.)

The intentional tort of *fraud* occurs when: (1) the defendant intentionally (or with reckless disregard for the truth) makes a false or misleading material assertion; (2) the plaintiff reasonably relies on the assertion; and (3) the plaintiff suffers damages caused by the misrepresentation. When a plaintiff enters into a contract based on the defendant's fraud, the contract is voidable on the plaintiff's part (*see Contracts*).

Red Flag Situation

Situation: A salesperson for a homebuilder tells a prospective buyer the central heating system in a new home is completely adequate for the winter temperatures. The salesperson knows the statement is false but there is no way the buyer can confirm the statement. The following winter, the new homeowner learns the heating system is completely inadequate for normal winter temperatures when the pipes in the home burst due to the cold temperatures, causing extensive damage.

Potential Problem: The homeowner can sue for the intentional tort of fraud: (1) the salesperson knowingly made a false statement; (2) the statement was a material assertion; (3) the homeowner was reasonable in relying on the statement; and (4) the homeowner suffered damages. Based on agency law, an employer is liable for torts committed by an employee "within the scope of employment." In this case, the homebuilder also faces tort liability.

Going Global

Tort laws vary throughout the world. In many countries, fraud is considered a serious crime and carries with it severe sanctions.

Reducing Your Risks

1. If you have sales agents working for you, make certain they understand the serious consequences of fraud. Sometimes a statement a salesperson considered as "sales talk" or "puffing" is later determined to be a factual assertion by a jury.

2. In order to sue for fraud, the plaintiff must prove the reliance on the false statement was justified. If you are purchasing goods from another party, for example, you may not be able to later sue for fraud claiming the seller misrepresented the condition of the goods if you were able to see the defects before the purchase.

Sources of Information

1. For more information on fraud, visit *http://www.law.cornell.edu/topics/torts.html*.

2. More information is available at *http://www.swlearning.com/blaw/fundamentals/fundamentals6e/fundamentals6e.html*. Go to "Interactive Study Center" and click on Chapter 4, "Torts and Cyber Torts."

$$Gg$$

Gift

(For additional information, *see Property*.)

A *gift* is a means of conveying property (real or personal) from the donor (the party giving the gift) to the donee (the recipient). In order for a gift to be valid, three requirements must be met: (1) the donor intended to make a gift (referred to as donative intent); (2) constructive or actual delivery of the gift; and (3) acceptance by the donee. A frequent reason for a gift to be determined invalid is lack of delivery.

There are two categories of gifts. A gift *inter vivos* is an unconditional gift. A gift *causa mortis* is a conditional gift made when the donor expects to die from an imminent illness, procedure or event. If the donor survives the illness, procedure or event, the gift is considered revoked.

Red Flag Situation

Situation: A philanthropist, facing heart surgery, tells the curator of an art museum, "Because I don't think I'll survive this surgery, I want the museum to have my art collection." The curator immediately plans an exhibit of the art that same day. The philanthropist survives.

Potential problem: The gift was a conditional gift *causa mortis*. The donor survived the surgery that prompted him to make the gift. The gift is thereby revoked.

Going Global

The requirements for a valid gift vary in different countries. In some countries, gifts of certain types of property must be evidence by a writing in order to be enforceable.

Reducing Your Risks

1. Understand the requirements for a valid gift. In order to claim a tax deduction for a gift to a charity, for instance, your business must meet the legal requirements for a valid gift.

2. Whether your business is the donor or the donee of a gift abroad, make certain the host country's legal requirements for a gift are met.

3. If the gift involves real property (land and its fixtures), a deed must be executed.

Sources of Information

1. To learn more about gifts and other means of conveying property, visit *http://www.law.cornell.edu/property*.

2. More information is available at *http://www.swlearning.com/blaw/ fundamentals/fundamentals6e/fundamentals6e.html*. Go to "Interactive Study Center" and click on Chapter 28, "Personal Property and Bailments."

Guaranty Contract

(For additional information, *see Surety*.)

In a *guaranty contract*, a third party (the guarantor) agrees to fulfill the obligation of the original promisor if that party defaults. The guarantor is thereby secondarily liable on the contract. As a general rule, the guaranty contract comes under the *Statute of Frauds* and therefore has to be in writing. An exception to this requirement occurs when the main purpose of the guaranty contract is to benefit the guarantor (referred to as the "main purpose rule.")

Red Flag Situation

Situation: An electronics store sells an expensive electronic system to a customer on credit. Concerned about the customer's creditworthiness, the store demands a guarantor in case the customer defaults. The customer's wealthy father-in-law verbally agrees to serve as guarantor as a favor to his son-in-law. The customer defaults after two payments.

Potential problem: According to the Statute of Frauds, a guaranty contract must be in writing unless it comes under the "main purpose rule." In this situation, the electronics store did not require a writing; therefore the verbal promise is unenforceable.

Going Global

The laws regarding which contracts must be in writing vary throughout the world. Many countries require any promise to be secondarily liable for another's debt must be in writing.

Reducing Your Risks

1. Make certain that your employees who may be involved in guaranty contracts understand the requirement for a writing.

2. If you enter into guaranty contracts in other countries, become familiar with the writing requirements in the host country.

3. Understand the requirements for a valid contract in any country where you will be doing business.

Sources of Information

1. Additional information is available at *http://www.law.cornell.edu/topics/ contracts.html.*

2. Also go to *http://www.swlearning.com/blaw/fundamentals/fundamentals6e/ fundamentals6e.html.* Click on "Interactive Study Center" and go to Chapter 10, "Defenses Against Contract Enforcement."

Hh

Holder in Due Course

(For additional information, *see Negotiable Instruments* and *Contracts*.)

The term *holder in due course (HDC)* refers to the holder of a negotiable instrument who can actually get better rights against the maker or drawer of the instrument than the party who transferred the instrument. Certain defenses the maker/drawer can raise against the party who transferred the instrument to the HDC cannot be raised against the HDC.

Businesses that are engaged in the purchase of negotiable instruments (for example, businesses that purchase promissory notes that are due at a later date) need to be very careful to assure that they qualify as an HDC.

Qualifications for an HDC: According to the Uniform Commercial Code (UCC), a holder in due course is the holder of an instrument if:

1. The instrument when issued or negotiated to the holder does not bear such apparent evidence of forgery or alternation or is not otherwise so irregular or incomplete as to call into question its authenticity; and

2. The holder took the instrument (i) for value; (ii) in good faith; and (iii) without notice that the instrument is overdue or has been dishonored or that there is an uncured default with respect to payment of another instrument issued as part of

the same series, (iv) without notice that the instrument contains an unauthorized signature or has been altered. In addition, the UCC requires the HDC had no notice of a claim to or defense against the instrument. (UCC 3-302) (To read the complete UCC provisions, please see http://www.law.cornell.edu/ucc/ucc.table.html.)

Defenses that are not Valid against an HDC: As mentioned above, an HDC takes the instrument "free from" certain defenses that the maker/drawer can raise against other parties as valid defenses for nonpayment. These defenses are referred to as "personal defenses."

Personal defenses include the following:

1. Breach of warranty or breach of the underlying contract. Assume a computer manufacturer sells a mainframe computer to an accounting firm on credit. The firm executes a promissory note. The manufacturer then sells the note to a finance company for immediate cash in order buy additional equipment. The finance company qualifies as an HDC. The accounting firm discovers the computer is defective and therefore the sales warranty is breached. The firm would have a valid defense (breach of warranty) for refusing to pay the computer manufacturer. The defense is not valid against an HDC and the accounting firm must therefore pay the finance company. The firm's only recourse is to sue the computer manufacturer for damages.

2. Failure of consideration or lack of consideration. Assume a horse farm promises to deliver a thoroughbred to a buyer. The buyer executes a negotiable instrument to the farm. The farm owner negotiates the instrument to a holder in due course. The horse is never delivered. The buyer would have a valid defense for not paying the note when it became due based on failure of consideration (the failure to deliver the horse). The buyer must pay the holder in due course, however, because failure of consideration is a personal defense.

3. Fraud in the inducement. Assume an art dealer assures a hotel that a painting is an original work of art. The hotel executes a negotiable instrument, takes the painting for display in its lobby and then learns it is a fake. The hotel has a valid defense for not paying the dealer but must honor the instrument vis-à-vis the holder in due course.

4. Illegality (if it would render the underlying contract voidable).

5. Mental incapacity of the maker/drawer if the party has not been adjudicated insane. (If a party has been adjudicated insane, the contract is void.)

In addition to the above, other personal defenses include duress and undue influence that make a contract voidable; nondelivery of the negotiable instrument; discharge of the instrument by cancellation or payment; and completing an incomplete instrument without authority.

Defenses that are valid against holder in due course: Certain defenses that a maker or drawer of a negotiable instrument can raise for not honoring the instrument are valid against a holder in due course; this means that the HDC cannot force the maker or drawer to pay. These defenses are referred to as universal or real defenses. They include the following:

1. Forgery of the maker's/drawer's signature.

2. Bankruptcy discharge for the maker/drawer.

3. Mental incapacity when the maker/drawer has been adjudicated insane.

4. Duress that is so extreme that it renders the instrument void.

5. A material alteration of the instrument.

6. An illegality that renders the transaction supporting the instrument void.

7. Fraud in the execution of the instrument.

Assume a salesperson approaches a visually impaired individual and asks the individual to sign a document. The salesperson states the document is a petition for a new stop light in town. The individual signs the document and 90 days later learns the document was a promissory note for $50,000. The holder in due course of the note demands payment. This is an example of fraud in the execution—the victim never intended to sign the note. In this case, the victim does not have to pay.

Red Flag Situation

Situation: An employee approaches the storeowner and requests the latter sign a document. Knowing the owner is near-sighted and not wearing glasses, the employee assures the owner the document is a get-well card for another worker. The owner signs the document without seeing what he has signed. Six months later, a holder in due course presents the owner with a promissory note for $50,000 bearing the owner's signature. The owner claims fraud in the execution. ***Potential Problem:*** When the maker's/drawer's own negligence resulted in signing a document without understanding the contents, courts have held the maker/drawer is liable on the instrument. In this situation, the storeowner should have taken the time to put on eyeglasses and read the document before signing it.

8. Minority of the maker/drawer if the state law provides that minority is a defense to the contract.

Red Flag Situation

Situation: A retail store sells a television set to a consumer on credit. The consumer executes a promissory note for $500. The store immediately sells the negotiable instrument to a finance company for $450. The television set was defective and the consumer refuses to continue payments. The finance company qualifies as an HDC and claims the consumer's defense for nonpayment (breach of warranty) is a personal defense and therefore not valid against a HDC.

Potential problem: As a general rule, personal defenses are not valid against a HDC and the maker/drawer must honor the instrument. An exception to this rule applies to sales of consumer goods. A rule passed by the Federal Trade Commission provides that any defense a consumer can raise against the original party to a contract for consumer goods is also valid against an HDC. In this case, the finance company cannot force the consumer to pay. The finance company's only recourse is to sue the retail store.

Going Global

1. In many international sales transactions, the negotiable instrument referred to as a banker's acceptance is frequently used. This instrument is a draft wherein a commercial bank is both the drawee and the acceptor of the instrument.

2. The negotiable instrument referred to as a draft in the U.S. is called a bill of exchange in many other countries.

3. The United Nations Convention on International Bills of Exchange and International Promissory Notes has been adopted in over 20 countries to define the rights and duties of parties to these types of instruments.

Reducing Your Risks

1. If your business is the payee of instruments (drafts, checks, promissory notes, trade acceptances), make certain the instrument qualifies as a negotiable instrument. This is especially important if you plan to negotiate the instrument to another party.

2. Understand the requirements to be met in order to qualify as an HDC whenever you obtain a negotiable instrument. As an HDC, you can have better rights to the instrument than the transferor of the document. (Certain defenses that the maker/drawer can raise for not paying the transferor are not valid against a HDC.)

3. Never sign a document without reading and understanding it. Courts have held that a party who unknowingly signs a negotiable instrument is liable if the maker/drawer failed to exercise diligence in the signing.

Sources of Information

1. For more information on the UCC, visit *http://www.law.cornell.edu/ucc*.

2. Visit *http://www.swlearning.com/blaw/fundamentals/fundamentals6e/fundamentals6e.html*. Click on "Interactive Study Center" and go to Chapter 18, "Negotiability, Transferability, and Liability."

Ii

Implied Warranties

Implied warranties automatically go with a sale, requiring no specific assurances on the seller's part. Article 2 of the Uniform Commercial (UCC) provides for certain types of implied warranties.

Implied Warranties created under Article 2 of the UCC:

1. *Implied Warranty of Merchantability*
   This warranty arises when the seller or lessor of goods is a merchant. According to the UCC (Article 2-104), a merchant is a person who deals in that particular type or goods or who holds oneself out as having expert knowledge or skill relative to that type of goods.

Unless the warranty has been excluded or modified, the UCC (Article 2-314(2)) provides that merchantable goods must:

(a) pass without objection in the trade under the contract description; and

(b) in the case of fungible goods, are of fair average quality within the description; and

(c) are fit for the ordinary purposes for which such goods are used; and

(d) run, within the variations permitted by the agreement of even kind, quality and quantity within each unit and among all units involved; and

(e) are adequately contained, packaged, and labeled as the agreement may require; and

(f) conform to the promises or affirmations of fact made on the container or label if any.

This warranty applies to the selling of food or drink whether the purchaser consumed the goods at the seller's premises or elsewhere (Article 2-314(1)),

2. *Implied Warranty of Fitness for a Particular Purpose*
According to Article 2-315, this warranty arises when "the seller at the time of contracting has reason to know any particular purpose for which the goods are required and that the buyer is relying on the seller's skill or judgment to select or furnish suitable goods, there is unless excluded or modified...an implied warranty that the goods shall be fit for such purpose."

3. *Implied Warranties Based on Course of Dealing or Trade Usage*
The UCC also recognizes implied warranties that may arise based on custom in the trade or a pattern of dealing established between the parties in the past.

Red Flag Situations

1. *Situation:* A major retail chain sells a large volume of designer umbrellas manufactured abroad. A number of customers complain after discovering the umbrellas are not water repellant.
Potential Problem: The sale of the umbrellas by a merchant seller carries with it the implied warranty of merchantability. A merchantable umbrella must therefore be fit for its ordinary purpose of protecting the user from rain. The retailer is therefore liable for breach of the implied warranty of merchantability.

2. *Situation:* A retail grocer sells canned mushrooms in the store. A customer buys a can and discovers small rocks among the mushrooms.
Potential Problem: The merchant grocer may be liable for breach of the implied warranty of merchantability. According to Article 2 of the UCC, if an item is found in food or drink, which is unexpected, the foods or drink is not merchantable. (In contrast, courts have held that if an item may naturally occur and is to be expected, such as a small bone in a fish, the food may still be considered merchantable.)

3. *Situation:* An office manager informs an electronics salesperson that the office needs a scanner that will allow scanned documents to be copied onto a disk and thereby transferred onto a computer. The salesperson selects a scanner for the buyer. Later the buyer discovers the scanner does not have these capabilities.

Potential Problem: Although the scanner may be merchantable (fit for its ordinary purposes), it breaches the implied warranty of fitness for the particular purpose of the buyer.

Going Global

1. Article 35 of the United Nations Convention on the International Sale of Goods (CISG) recognizes implied warranties very similar to those discussed above. These include the implied warranty of fitness for a particular purpose and the implied warranty of fitness for the ordinary purpose.

2. Consumer laws regarding the creation of implied warranties vary throughout the world. If you are selling goods to a foreign buyer, understand how an implied warranty is created.

3. Many countries do not require a writing for a contract to be enforceable. To make certain both parties understand what warranties are included in the contract, a writing is still advisable.

Reducing Your Risks

1. Understand how an implied warranty is created domestically and abroad. Remember that an implied warranty requires no specific affirmation on the seller's or lessor's part.

2. Caution your sales force about the risk involved in selecting goods for a buyer's particular needs. Even though the goods are merchantable, the buyer may later claim they do not meet the particular needs of the buyer.

Sources of Information

1. For more information on the CISG, visit *http://www.cisg.law.pace.edu.*

2. A Businessperson's Guide to Warranties is available from the Federal Trade Commission at *http://www.ftc.gov/bcp/conline/pubs/buspubs/warranty.*

3. To learn more about implied warranties, go to *http://www.swlearning.com/blaw/ fundamentals/ fundamentals6e/fundamentals6e.html.* Click on "Internet Study Center" and then Chapter 17, "Warranties and Product Liability."

Intentional Infliction of Emotional Distress

(For additional information, *see Torts.*)

The tort of *intentional infliction of emotional distress* occurs when the defendant engages in an outrageous activity intended to cause the plaintiff to suffer a high degree of emotional distress. The courts are beginning to recognize this behavior as an actionable tort more frequently as it becomes easier for the plaintiff to prove the physical and psychological damage resulting from the mental distress.

This tort can occur both within and outside the workplace. Assume a long-time employee loses out to a newer employee for a promotion. Blaming the supervisor who recommended the newer employee for the promotion, the disgruntled employee makes an anonymous call to the supervisor, informing the supervisor that a close family member has been seriously injured. The information is false, and the purpose of the call is solely to inflict emotional distress upon the supervisor. The supervisor can successfully sue the caller for intentional infliction of emotional distress.

An increasing number of claims based on this tort are also being brought by employees charging supervisors with intentionally inflicting emotional distress in order to create a hostile work environment and thereby forcing the employee to resign.

Another example of this tort occurring in the workplace involved a case where a restaurant manager announced that employees would be fired in alphabetical order until the identity of an alleged thief within the workplace was revealed. The employee whose last name started with "A" successfully sued the manager for intentional infliction of emotional distress based on the apprehension suffered in anticipation of being fired.

Red Flag Situation

Situation: For personal reasons, a supervisor wants a particular employee to resign. The current employee has a good work record and the supervisor has no valid grounds for dismissing the worker. Attempting to force the employee to resign, the supervisor regularly harasses and embarrasses the employee in the presence of others.

Potential Problem: The employee may sue the supervisor for intentional infliction of emotional distress. In addition, the employer may also be liable for the supervisor's tort because the tort was committed within the scope of employment. (For additional information on employer liability, *see Agency.*)

Lawsuits based on intentional infliction of emotional distress are also being brought by debtors against companies involved in debt collection. The debtor may claim the debt collector intentionally engaged in practices intended to cause the debtor to suffer emotionally. (For additional information on potential liability in the debt collection process, *see Fair Debt Collection Practices Act.*)

In some states, stalking another person can lead to liability for this intentional tort in addition to the criminal liability imposed.

Going Global

Tort laws vary greatly through the world. In recent years an increasing number of foreign legal systems have begun to recognize certain forms of outrageous behavior in the workplace as actionable torts.

Reducing Your Risks

1. If your company is involved in debt collection, make certain that company employees refrain from extreme actions in their collection practices. If a collection procedure is deemed outrageous, the debtor may sue for intentional infliction of emotional distress.

2. Make certain that supervisors do not harass, intimidate or participate in other intentional activities that may cause an employee to suffer from emotional distress. The employer can be liable for this tort if a court determines the tort was committed within the scope of employment.

Sources of Information

1. For additional information on this and other torts, visit *http://www.swlearning.com/ blaw/fundamentals/fundamentals6e/ fundamentals6e.html*. Go to "Court Case Updates" and then go to "Torts."

2. More information is available at the above Web site by clicking on "Interactive Study Center" and then Chapter 4, "Torts and Cybertorts."

Innkeeper's Liability

(For additional information, *see Bailments.*)

The term *innkeeper's liability* refers to the liability an innkeeper (an owner of an inn, hotel or motel) incurs in the event a guest's personal property is damaged or lost. At one time an innkeeper was strictly liable for any loss a guest sustained. Today, most states have statutes providing the innkeeper is not strictly liable if certain statutory requirements are met. (The innkeeper still faces potential liability if there was negligence involved.) As a general rule, the statutes require the innkeeper to provide a safe for keeping guests' personal items. In addition, the innkeeper must inform the guests in writing of the availability of the safe and the writing must be posted in a specific place in the guest room.

Red Flag Situations

1. **Situation:** An innkeeper is not familiar with the state statute that requires posting a notice in a specific location informing guests of the available of a safe. A guest discovers an expensive ring left in the room is missing.
   Potential Problem: By failing to comply with the state law, the innkeeper may be strictly liable for the lost ring.

2. **Situation:** A company pays for permanent housing accommodations for a key executive in a downtown hotel.
   Potential Problem: As a permanent resident, the executive may be considered a "lodger" in the hotel rather than a "guest." In this situation, the innkeepers' potential strict liability does not apply because the executive is a lodger. The executive should therefore make certain that there is adequate individual insurance to cover a lodger's personal property in the hotel.

Going Global

Laws regarding innkeeper's liability vary throughout the world. Many laws impose specific responsibilities on innkeepers regarding the safekeeping of guests' personal items. In addition, guests must comply with the law in order to hold the innkeeper liable for personal items lost or damaged in the inn.

Reducing Your Risks

1. If your company operates inns, hotels, or motels, make certain the properties are in compliance with state laws regarding innkeeper's liability in each state of operation.

2. Advise your employees who travel for the company to become familiar with the duties of guests relevant to the safekeeping of personal items, including computers and cell phones.

3. If your company provides permanent living facilities in inns, hotels, or motels for employees, determine whether the employee is considered a guest or a lodger. If the employee is a lodger, additional insurance covering the lodger's personal property may be needed.

4. Whether your traveling employee is a guest or a lodger, advise the traveler on obtaining personal property insurance to cover loss or damage the property may sustain in an innkeeper's facility.

Sources of Information

1. To learn more about innkeeper's liability, go to *http://www.swlearning.com/ blaw/fundamentals/fundamentals6e/fundamentals6e.html*. Go to "Court Case Updates" and click on "Real and Personal Property."

Insider Trading

The term ***insider trading*** refers to violating a duty to the company issuing the securities by engaging in the selling or buying of securities based on information the trader possesses that is unavailable to the general public.

Applicable Law: The Securities Exchange Act of 1934 (17 C.F.R. 240) (the Act) regulates the securities exchanges as well as security brokers and dealers. Section 10b-5 and Section 16(b) of the Act pertain to insider trading.

Section 10b-5: This section of the Act makes it illegal to engage in fraud when buying or selling a security. This section is also the basis for the Securities and Exchange Commission (SEC) Rule 10b-5, which states:

"It shall be unlawful for any person, directly or indirectly, by use of any means or instrumentality of interstate commerce or of the mails, or of any facility of any national securities exchange,

a. to employ any device, scheme, or artifice to defraud,

b. to make any untrue statement of a material fact or to omit to state a material fact necessary in order to make the statements made, in the light of the circumstances under which they were made, not misleading, or

c. to engage in any act, practice, or course of business that operates or would operate as a fraud or deceit upon any person, in connection with the purchase or sale of any security."

This rule applies to virtually any security transaction, including private transactions. It further applies to most types of securities, including bonds, notes, profit sharing agreements and agreements to form corporations.

Parties Subject to Rule 10b-5: The rule applies not only to corporate insiders (such as directors, officers and majority shareholders) but also to certain parties outside the corporation who gain access to the information and trade on it.

Theories for Applying Rule 10b-5: The courts have adopted two theories for holding outsiders liable for trading on inside information. These are referred to as the

Tipper/Tippee Theory and the Misappropriation Theory.

Liability based on the Tipper/Tippee Theory: An outsider (tippee) can be liable for insider trading when the tippee obtains information from a corporate insider (tipper) who breaches a fiduciary duty to the corporation by disclosing the information. In addition, if the tippee passes on the information to another party, the latter party may also be liable as a "tippee of the tippee."

Red Flag Situations

1. *Situation:* A corporate executive tells a friend at a social event that the executive's company will soon be taken over by a large conglomerate. The information is not available to the public. The executive and the friend each purchase 1000 shares of the target company the next day. Following the takeover, the target company's stock doubles in value.
   Potential Problem: Both parties may be liable for insider trading based on the "tipper/tippee" theory.

2. *Situation:* A shareholder in a major petroleum company learns from a corporate executive that the company's latest foreign drilling project has turned up "dry" and the company will lose millions of dollars. The information has not been released to the public. The executive and the shareholder sell all of their stock before the information becomes public and the stock sinks in value.
   Potential Problem: The executive and the shareholder can be liable for insider trading based on the "tipper/tippee" theory. The theory applies to both the purchase of stock and the sale of stock based on insider information.

Liability Based on the Misappropriation Theory: Insider trading liability can be imposed on a party who is not a corporate insider if that party has access to inside information and misappropriates that information. The following situation provides an example.

Red Flag Situation

Situation: An accountant with a major firm is retained to prepare the financial papers necessary for a major corporate takeover. The accountant buys 1,000 shares of the target company before the takeover is announced. Following the takeover, the target company's stock doubles in value.
Potential Problem: According to the "misappropriation theory," a court may determine the accountant owed fiduciary duties of nondisclosure (of the client's information) both to the accountant's employer (the accounting firm) and to the client. The accountant can be held liable for insider trading based on the misappropriation theory.

Sanctions Under Rule 10b-5 and the Sarbanes-Oxley Act:

1. Criminal Sanctions: Intentional violation of Rule 10b-5 is considered a crime. Criminal penalties include up to 25 years in prison and/or up to $5 million in fines for an individual. A business entity may be fined up to $25 million. *Note:* The Sarbanes-Oxley Act of 2002 raised the imprisonment term from 20 years to 25 years.

2. Civil Sanctions: A defendant individual or business may also be subject to civil sanctions and required to pay monetary damages.

Lawsuits Brought By the SEC: According to the Insider Trading Sanctions Act of 1984, the SEC may sue certain insider traders in federal court if the transaction was through a broker/dealer or a national security exchange.

Lawsuits Brought By Private Parties: Private parties (individuals and businesses) injured by insider trading can bring suit in federal civil courts.

State Securities Laws: Many state laws are based on Rule 10b-5 and securities traders are subject to both federal and state securities laws.

Section 16(b) Liability: This provision of the Act applies to any officer, director, or shareholder owning at least 10% of the securities in a company. The provision prohibits any of the above parties from buying and then selling or selling and then buying back the corporation's securities within a six-month period. The corporation can recapture any "short-swing" profits realized in such a transaction. An insider in violation of the section can be sued by the shareholders or by the corporation. Certain transactions are exempt from this rule.

Red Flag Situation

Situation: A shareholder owning 15 percent of the corporation's equities buys an additional 1,000 shares on January 15. On March 15 the shareholder sells the 1,000 shares, realizing a profit of $5,000. At no time did the shareholder have access to any inside information to influence the purchase or sale.

Potential Problem: According to Section 16(b), the shareholder may be sued by either the corporation or other shareholders for the "short-swing" profit realized in the sale of the stock in less than six months after their purchase. It is immaterial that the defendant did not trade on any inside information.

Going Global

Securities laws, including those addressing insider trading, vary greatly throughout the world. In some countries sanctions imposed for insider trading are much harsher than in this country.

Reducing Your Risks

1. If your company is involved in any form of securities trading (including profit-sharing agreements) make certain that all parties with access to inside information understand the potential liability under Rule 10b-5.

2. If your company provides services (such as accounting, computer, legal, engineering) to clients that trade in securities, familiarize your employees with the misappropriation theory as it applies to insider trading.

3. Review state securities laws that may impact your company in intrastate transactions.

4. Keep in mind that securities laws (including the laws relating to insider trading) are complex and it is advisable to seek counsel before engaging in any activities involving trading in securities.

Sources of Information

1. For more information on the Securities Exchange Act of 1934, visit the University of Cincinnati College of Law's Center for Corporate Law at *http://www.law.uc.edu/ccl*.

2. The Securities and Exchange Commission discusses insider trading. Go to *http://www.sec.gov*.

3. More information is available at *http://www.swlearning.com/blaw/fundamentals/fundamentals6e/fundamentals6e.html*. Go to "Interactive Study Center" and click on Chapter 27, "Investor Protection and Online Securities Offerings."

Insurance

(For information on specific types of insurance, *see Life Insurance; Liability Insurance; Property Insurance; Title Insurance; Vehicle Insurance; and Workers' Compensation Insurance*.)

The term ***insurance*** refers to a ***contract*** (policy) where the insurer promises to reimburse the insured (or a third party beneficiary) in the event the insured suffers specified losses. In exchange for the protection, the insured agrees to make stated premium payments to the insurer while the policy is in force. Insurance law requires that the insured have an insurable interest in the person or property covered. In order to have an insurable interest, the insured must prove the insured will suffer a loss in the event of a death (in a life insurance policy) or damage to property (in a property policy). Insurance is frequently referred to as a form of risk shifting.

Specific Provisions in an Insurance Policy: Among the provisions found in a typical insurance policy are the following:

1. Effective date of coverage: A policy may state that coverage begins immediately or at some date in the future. The insured may request protection between the time the first premium is paid and the insurer actually issues the policy. This protection is in the form of a binder.

2. Co-insurance clause: A property insurance policy may require the insured retain coverage adequate to cover a specified percentage of the property. A policy, for example, may require the insured's policy cover at least 80% of the property's value in order for the insured to recover the full face value of the policy if a total loss of property occurs.

3. Cancellation clause: A state law may limit the reasons for which the insured can cancel a policy.

4. Arbitration clause: Many policies include an ***arbitration*** clause requiring the parties submit any dispute to binding arbitration rather than filing a lawsuit.

5. Pre-existing condition: Health and life insurance policies may provide there will not be coverage for a loss due to a health condition existing at the time the policy is issued until a specified period of time passes.

Red Flag Situation

Situation: A company has a property insurance policy on its multi-million dollar manufacturing plant. The policy has a co-insurance clause requiring the policy cover at least 80 percent of the property value. The company has not had the property appraised recently and is unaware the property value increased by 10 percent in the past year. A fire completely destroys the plant.

Potential problem: Due to the 10 percent increase in property value, the insured should have requested an increase in insurance coverage in order to meet the 80 percent requirement. By failing to increase the coverage, the company will not be able to obtain the full face value of the policy.

Going Global

1. Companies with overseas operations may benefit from obtaining political risk insurances to cover such risks as currency inconvertibility, expropriation, revolution, and insurrections. This type of insurance is available from the national agency, the Overseas Private Investment Corporation (OPIC), as well as from private companies. For more information on OPIC's coverage, visit

http://www.opic.gov.

2. A major concern for companies shipping cargo overseas is the risk of loss of damage during shipment. For information on marine cargo insurance, visit the site for the National Customs Brokers and Forwarders Association of American at *http://www.NCBFAA.org.*

3. Insurance laws vary throughout the world. Become familiar with the insurance laws of the host country and make certain your activities abroad are adequately protected.

Reducing Your Risks

1. Determine if the appraisal of your business property is current. If your property insurance policy includes a co-insurance clause, make certain your current coverage meets the percentage required in the clause.

2. Make certain that employees who drive company vehicles have good driving records. Employing drivers with poor records increases the company's premiums.

3. Insist on a title policy any time your company purchases real estate.

4. Consider the merits of obtaining life insurance policies on key employees of the company. Losing a key person can result in significant loss to the business.

5. If your company's facilities (office building, plant, etc.) will be vacant at any time, notify the insurer of this fact. The current policy may provide coverage only if the facility is occupied. Additional premiums may be required to assure coverage while the facility is unoccupied.

Sources of Information

1. To learn about vehicle insurance in different states, go to *http://www.autoinsurancelaw.com/*, click on "Insurance Laws,"and then click on the state.

2. More information is available at *http://www.swlearning.com/blaw/ fundamentals/fundamentals6e/fundamentals6e.html.* Go to "Interactive Study Center" and click on Chapter 30, "Insurance, Wills and Trusts."

Intellectual Property

(For information on specific types of intellectual property, *see Copyrights, Patents, Trademarks,* and *Trade Secrets*.)

The term *intellectual property* refers to intangible personal property which results from one's intellectual endeavors. A holder of intellectual property may bring a lawsuit for infringement against one who improperly uses the property. Examples of intellectual property include *Copyrights, Patents, Trademarks* and *Trade Secrets*.

Interstate Commerce Clause

The Interstate Commerce Clause of the U.S. Constitution provides that Congress shall have the power "To regulate Commerce with foreign Nations, and among the several States, and with the Indian Tribes;" (Article 1, Section 8).

The Clause and the Civil Rights Act of 1964: Based on the interstate commerce clause, the courts have held Congress has the power to regulate even businesses that operate solely within one state because the local business is still involved in some form of interstate commerce. For example, the U.S. Supreme Court ruled that the federal Civil Rights Act of 1964 prohibiting businesses from discriminating based on race applied to a small local motel in Georgia. The court reasoned that the motel's operation was not strictly local because it was accessible from interstate highways, advertised nationally, and its guests were from other states and countries.

The Clause and Antitrust Law: A local real estate board in Louisiana was charged with violating the federal Sherman Antitrust Act by price setting of real estate commission rates. The defendant claimed there was no interstate activity involved and therefore the Act did not apply. The U.S. Supreme Court ruled the real estate board was involved in interstate commerce because title policies were issued by companies in other states; buyers and sellers were from out of state and the lending institutions providing the purchase monies were located out of state.

Red Flag Situation

Situation: A large restaurant employing 100 employees has only one place of business. The restaurant establishes a policy of refusing to hire any applicant over 40 years of age. A qualified applicant, age 41, is turned down for a position based strictly on age. The applicant threatens to file a claim based on the federal Age Discrimination in Employment Act. The restaurant claims it is not engaged in interstate commerce and therefore is not subject to federal legislation including the Age

Discrimination in Employment Act.

Potential problem: A court will determine that the business is engaged in interstate commerce based on the fact its customers are from other states and countries; it accommodates those traveling on the interstate highways; and it purchases products and supplies produced in other states and countries. It is therefore subject to the federal law protecting workers 40 years old and older from discrimination.

Going Global

As noted above, the Interstate Commerce Clause provides Congress can regulate commerce with foreign nations. U. S. businesses involved in transactions with parties in other countries are therefore subject to federal regulations and laws.

Reducing Your Risks

1. Do not assume that your business is not subject to federal laws and regulations because the business is strictly local in its operations. Today the courts are holding that virtually all business in the U.S. are in some way involved in interstate commerce.

2. Keep in mind that interstate commerce is involved in a transaction between a U.S. business and a member of a U.S. Indian tribe.

Sources of Information

1. For additional information on the U.S. Constitution, visit *http://www.law.cornell.edu/constitution/constitution.overview.html.*

2. To learn more, go to *http://www.swlearning.com/blaw/fundamentals/ fundamentals6e/fundamentals6e.html.* Then go to "Court Case Updates" and click on "Constitutional Law."

Jj

Joint and Several Liability

(For additional information, *see Partnership*.)

The term *joint and several liability* provides that a plaintiff with a claim against a general partnership for debts, breach of contract, or tort may "severe off" one individual general partner to sue rather than suing all of the partners or the partnership itself. According to the Revised Uniform Partnership Act, before a creditor can sue the individual partners of a solvent partnership, the creditor must first try to collect from the partnership or must satisfy a court that an attempt to collect would be futile (Section 307d).

Red Flag Situation

Situation: One partner in a general partnership enters into a contract to purchase $50,000 in inventory. The other general partner is out of the country at the time of contracting. The company that sold the inventory is unable to collect the $50,000 from the partnership.

Potential Problem: If the state in which the suit is brought has adopted the RUPA, the plaintiff creditor can "severe" off and name only the partner who was out of the country at the time of contracting. If the plaintiff wins, the partner named in the lawsuit can seek indemnification from the other partner.

State Law and Joint and Several Liability: A majority of states have now adopted the RUPA. In those states that still follow the original Uniform Partnership Act (UPA), there may be joint liability (rather than joint and several liability) for partnership contracts and debts. In that case, the plaintiff creditor must name all the partners. The partners still face joint and several liability for tort claims against the partnership. In some states, the plaintiff may sue the partnership itself, thereby binding the partnership's assets as well as the partners' individual assets.

Going Global

Partnership laws vary throughout the world. Many countries recognize the joint and several liability of general partners for the debts, contracts, and tort liability of the partnership entity.

Reducing Your Risks

1. Before becoming a partner in a general partnership, evaluate the potential risk of liability for the debts, contracts, and torts of the partnership. If your state has adopted the Revised Uniform Partnership Act, you may face joint and several liability for the partnership debts. In every state, you face joint and several liability for tort claims.

2. According to the RUPA, a creditor can choose to sue one or more general partners in their individual capacity if the creditor convinces a court trying to collect from the partnership (even though it is solvent) would be futile. It is therefore important to make certain the parties responsible for paying partnership debts do not block efforts of creditors to collect legitimate debts.

Sources of Information

1. To learn more about partnerships, go to *http://www.swlearning.com/blaw/fundamentals/fundamentals6e/fundamentals6e.html.* Click on "Interactive Study Guide" and then Chapter 24, "Sole Proprietorships, Partnerships, Limited Liability Companies, and Partnerships."

Joint Venture

(For additional information, *see Partnership.*)

A *joint venture* is basically a form of partnership that is created for a single project, transaction, or activity. For example, a partnership formed for the sole purpose of building a shopping mall may be considered a joint venture.

Ll

Landlord-Tenant Law

(For additional information, *see* **Contract**, **Landlord's Duty**, **Property**, and **Real Property Law**.)

Landlord–tenant law (the law) addresses the relationship between lessors and lessees of *real property*. Sources of law pertaining to the relationship include contract law, property law, and statutory law. This section relates to the lease of commercial property only.

Contract Law and the Landlord–Tenant Relationship: The rights and duties existing between the landlord and tenant are identified in the contract referred to as a lease. The lease must meet all the requirements of a contract in order to be valid. In most states, the *Statute of Frauds* requires that certain leases must be in writing to be enforceable. As a general rule, the lease includes a description of the property; the term of the lease; amount of rent; a provision transferring possession to the tenant; indication of the parties' intention to enter into a tenancy, and the landlord's right to repossess the property upon termination of the lease. In addition, the lease identifies the rights and duties of each party. In some states, the tenant cannot assign tenancy rights unless the lease provides for assignment. As with other contracts, a lease must be for a legal purpose in order to be valid. In certain states, topics to be included in a commercial lease are specified in the state statutes on property law.

Property Law and the Landlord–Tenant Relationship: When the lease contract and statutory law do not address a certain area of the relationship, common law property law may apply. Property law assures the tenant of the right of peaceable enjoyment of the property during the term of the lease. The tenant has the duty of taking reasonable care of the property. As a general rule, the tenant is not liable for the normal wear and tear of the property unless the lease specifies otherwise.

Statutory Law and the Landlord–Tenant Relationship: Local, state, and federal statutes are additional sources of landlord-tenant law.

Local Laws Applicable to Landlord-Tenant Relationships: Local statutes include city zoning regulations, city fire codes, and local building codes. For example, the Chicago City Council approved the High Rise Buildings – Emergency Procedures Ordinance soon after September 11, 2001. One provision of the ordinance requires owners of high-rise buildings to prepare and take steps to implement an emergency evacuation plan. The plan includes the names of designated and trained employees to assist in evacuation and a list of regular occupants who have identified themselves as needing assistance in the event of an evacuation and the type of assistance needed. Monthly building inspections are required to assure safe egress of the building. An amendment to the Chicago Building Code requires commercial buildings of a certain minimum height to install on-site diesel driven generators.

The city of Houston's Fire Department Standard 13-1 regarding high rise evacuation plan requires owners of high-rise buildings to have a Fire Safety Director who will provide proper training to staff, tenants, residents, and guests of the building in case of an emergency.

Owners and managers of commercial buildings are responsible for complying with all applicable city regulations.

State Laws Applicable to Landlord-Tenant Relationships: In addition to city ordinances, commercial landlords are subject to state regulations, including state fire codes, state property codes, and state health codes. For example, Chapter 93 of the Texas Property Code addresses commercial tenancies. The law provides that the landlord of commercial property cannot legally interrupt utility service paid directly to the utility company by the tenant unless there is a bona fide need for construction, repairs, or an emergency situation. In addition, the landlord cannot change the door lock of a commercial tenant who is late in paying rent. Also, the landlord must return a tenant's security deposit within a specified number of days unless the tenant has damaged the property.

Applicable Federal Laws: Federal laws applicable to the landlord-tenant relationship include anti-discrimination laws.

Red Flag Situations

1. ***Situation:*** A tenant in a commercial building is injured by a fire while working in the tenant's real estate office. The landlord had failed to install adequate exit lights as required by the state fire code.
   Potential Problem: The landlord may be liable for the tenant's injuries based on the negligence theory referred to as negligence per se. This theory is applied when the defendant (the landlord in this case) breaches a statute that carries with it a criminal penalty and the statute was passed to protect persons such as the plaintiff from the type of injury the plaintiff suffered.

2. ***Situation:*** A consulting firm enters into a contract to lease an historic old home to serve as its new office. Despite the fact the neighborhood is zoned for residential use only, the firm moves all of its furnishings into the historic structure.
   Potential Problem: Utilizing the building for commercial purposes violates the city zoning code and the lease is therefore not valid.

Going Global

1. Landlord-tenant laws vary greatly in other countries. Prospective lessees should become familiar with the host country's laws prior to entering into a lease agreement.

2. In many countries, formerly government-owned commercial properties are being privatized and sold to foreign investors who then lease the property to others. The host country's landlord-tenant laws may greatly expand the landlord's duties beyond the duties imposed in the U.S.

Reducing Your Risks

1. Insist on a written lease whether you are the landlord or tenant in a commercial rental agreement.

2. If you are a landlord, become familiar with applicable laws that impact your rights and duties under the lease agreement. Understand that you are subject to applicable local, state, and federal laws. Each of these can impose different responsibilities on the commercial landlord.

3. If you own commercial property, acquaint your agents with the formalities of the written notices that are required prior to evicting a tenant.

4. Review your state's laws regarding the handling and return of security deposits. Some states require the deposit be returned within a specified number of days from the lease termination or the renter must be notified in writing why the deposit is being detained.

5. Contract law provides that the injured party has the duty to mitigate damages. If a tenant breaches a lease and vacates, the landlord has the duty to make a good faith attempt to lease the premises to another tenant and thereby reduce the damages resulting from the breach.

Source of Information

1. The U.S. Department of Housing and Urban Development provides information on commercial property law at *http://www.hud.gov*.

2. Additional information on landlord/tenant relations is available at *http://www.law. cornell.edu/topics/landlord_tenant.html*.

3. Also visit *http://www.swlearning.com/blaw/fundamentals/fundamentals6e/ fundamentals6e.html*. Go to "Court Case Updates" and click on "Real and Personal Property."

Landowner's Duty

(For additional information, *see Negligence*.)

In the commercial setting, the ***landowner's duty*** includes a duty to provide safe and healthy premises for tenants and also to third parties coming onto the premises in certain situations. Failure to exercise reasonable care to protect persons coming onto the commercial property (referred to as "business invitees") from harm may result in liability for negligence. For the landowner to be held liable, the injured party must prove: (1) the landlord owed a duty of reasonable care to the plaintiff; (2) the landlord breached that duty; (3) the breach of duty was the actual and foreseeable cause; and (4) of the injuries plaintiff suffered.

Red Flag Situation

Situation: Several recent robberies have occurred in the area surrounding an all-night restaurant. A restaurant customer is robbed and injured in the poorly lit parking lot in front of the business.

Potential Problem: The property owner had a duty to provide adequate lighting (and possibly a security guard) to protect customers in the restaurant parking lot. The injured customer may successfully claim negligence based on the landowner's failure to provide safe parking facilities.

Going Global

Tort laws (including laws on negligence) vary greatly throughout the world. In many countries, landowners may be liable for injuries occurring to lessees and to third parties that result from the acts of third parties.

Reducing Your Risks

1. Understand that a landowner may be liable for injuries a business invitee sustains even when a third party stranger causes the injuries.

2. In some situations, trespassers have successfully sued landowners for injuries the trespasser sustained on the landowner's property. Certain courts have held that landowners owe a duty to all parties, including trespassers, to warn of certain dangers on the property.

3. Make certain that your business has adequate liability insurance to cover a claim brought by a party who incurs injury while on your real property.

Sources of Information

1. To learn more about negligence, visit the Internet Law Library at *http://www.lawguru.com/ilawlib*.

2. Additional information is available at *http://www.swlearning.com/blaw/fundamentals/fundamentals6e/fundamentals6e.html*. Go to "Court Case Updates" and click on "Torts."

Liability Insurance

(For additional information on the requirements and provisions of a typical insurance policy, *see Insurance*.)

The term *liability insurance* refers to the category of insurance that provides the insured with protection in case another party claims the insured is responsible for personal injury or property damage sustained by the other party.

Situations Where the Insured May be Liable for Another Party's Loss

The following are typical situations where the need for liability insurance may arise:

1. A company delivery vehicle is involved in a car accident and the other driver claims the delivery person caused the accident and sues the company.

2. A client slips and falls in the office of a financial brokerage firm. The client claims the injury was due to the slippery condition of the newly waxed floor and sues the firm.

3. An accountant is sued for malpractice (negligence) by a client.*

4. The members of the board of directors of a major corporation are sued by the shareholders for negligence in handling certain corporate matters. (Many board members today insist on the corporation purchasing liability insurance so the members may be indemnified for any costs sustained in a lawsuit arising from their corporate performance.)*

*Liability protection in these situations can be addressed by obtaining an ***errors and omission policy.*** In this type of policy, the insurer agrees to pay on the insured's behalf for damages (in excess of the stated deductible) arising from the insured's alleged negligence, error, or omission while engaged in performing professional duties. The policy may also provide the insurer will pay a certain amount for the days the insured appears in court and for any post-judgment interest arising from the judgment. As a general rule, the policy will not cover intentional acts on the insured's part such as fraud, libel, or discrimination.

Going Global

Insurance laws vary greatly throughout the world. Learn about the insurance laws of any host country where your company may be subject to a claim by another party for personal injuries or property damage.

Reducing Your Risks

1. If you plan to sit on the board of directors of any corporation, confirm the adequacy of your liability insurance in case of a lawsuit arising from your role as a director.

2. Before your company operates vehicles in this country or abroad, make certain your employees are covered by adequate liability insurance.

3. Review your liability insurance policies on a regular basis to confirm the coverage is adequate.

4. Understand that many liability policies on commercial buildings contain a pollution exclusion clause. If you own or manage commercial property and the guests or tenants may be exposed to chemicals, consider additional coverage to protect in case you are sued due to injuries relating to chemical exposure.

Sources of Information

1. Additional information on liability insurance is available from Cornell at *http://www.law.cornell.edu/topics/liabilityinsurance.html.*

2. Also visit *http://www.swlearning.com/blaw/fundamentals/fundamentals6e/ fundamentals6e.html.* Go to "Interactive Study Center" and click on Chapter 30, "Insurance, Wills, and Trusts."

Libel

(For additional information, *see **Defamation** and **Torts**.*)

The intentional tort of **libel** involves a false statement that injures the plaintiff's reputation. In the past, libel applied only to false and injurious statements that were written. Spoken statements could be the basis of a **slander** suit. Today, with the permanent preservation of spoken words through recordings (such as videotapes of television programming), libel may also apply to statements made verbally. For example, a plaintiff may bring a libel suit based on a statement made on a television talk show. The distinction between libel and slander is less pronounced today.

Requirements for Libel

In order for the plaintiff to prevail in a libel suit, the plaintiff must prove the following:

1. the defendant made a false statement;

2. the statement is harmful to plaintiff's reputation; and

3. the statement was published to at least one other person.
   The publication requirement is met when one other person (other than the parties to the lawsuit) reads or hears the statement. Courts have held that the defendant's dictation of the false and injurious statement to a secretary meets the publication requirement. If a third party overhears the defendant making the statement to the plaintiff, the publication requirement is also met.

Defenses

1. Truth is the ultimate defense in a defamation case.

2. Privilege refers to certain statements that, although defamatory, are protected. Protected statements include those made by attorneys in courtroom proceedings and statements made by members of the U.S. Congress during debate on the floors of Congress.

3. In addition, absence of malice is a defense when the plaintiff is a public figure. In

this situation, the plaintiff must prove malice on the defendant's part. Malice means that the defendant either (a) knew the statement was false or (b) made the statement with reckless disregard for the truth.

Red Flag Situation

Situation: A company manager sends e-mail to the head of Human Resources falsely accusing an employee of padding a travel expense account.

Potential Problem: The employee can sue for defamation because the false statement, harmful to plaintiff's reputation, was published to a third party (the head of Human Resources). The manager's employer can be held liable for the manager's tort because it was committed within the scope of employment. (For additional information, *see Agency*.)

Going Global

Defamation laws (including the laws regarding libel) vary throughout the world. Many other countries recognize the liability of the employer for the employee's tort committed within the scope of employment.

Reducing Your Risks

1. Understand that an injurious statement in an employee evaluation or in a letter of recommendation for a former employee may be the basis for a lawsuit based on libel. For this reason, many companies no longer provide former employees with letters of recommendation; the companies will only verify the time period when the former employee worked for the company.

2. Make certain the allegations are true before accusing an employee in writing (including via e-mail) of wrongdoing.

Sources of Information

1. To learn more about libel, visit the Internet Law Library at *http://www.lawguru.com/ilawlib*.

2. Additional information on libel and other torts is available at *http://www.law.cornell.edu/topics/torts.html*.

3. Also visit *http://www.swlearning.com/blaw/fundamentals/fundamentals6e/fundamentals6e.html*. Go to "Interactive Study Center" and click on Chapter 4, "Torts and Cybertorts."

Limited Liability Company

The term *limited liability company (LLC)* refers to a hybrid form of business organization that combines certain aspects of the corporate form of business with those of a partnership.

Advantages of the LLC: A major advantage of the LLC is the limited liability of the owners, who are referred to as managers. Their risk of loss is limited to their investment in the business. Another advantage available to LLCs with two or more managers is the opportunity to choose to be taxed either as a corporation or as a partnership. If the latter method of taxation is chosen, the managers can deduct business expenses and losses from their individual federal tax payments and avoid the double taxation applicable to corporations.

Disadvantages of the LLC: The LLC's existence is based on state statutes, which are not the same in each state. To be treated as an LLC, a business must therefore comply with the applicable statutes in the state of formation. These statutes require filing the Articles of Management with the proper state office and complying with all relevant state requirements.

The Filing Requirement: One state's LLC law requires a new LLC to publish a notice in two newspapers for six weeks. Following the publications, the LLC must file an affidavit with the State confirming the publications. A recent court case claimed these requirements violated the LLC owner's rights of due process and equal protection. The requirements were upheld by a state appellate court.

Possible Takeover of the LLC by a Bankruptcy Trustee: Another possible disadvantage involves an LLC that is comprised of only one member. A state court recently held that when the sole member of an LLC petitions for Chapter 7 personal bankruptcy, the entire LLC membership is passed on to the bankruptcy estate. As a result, the bankruptcy trustee can take control of the LLC, sell its real property, and apply the sales proceeds to the bankruptcy estate.

As mentioned previously, state laws on LLCs vary from state to state. Some states have adopted the Uniform Limited Liability Company Act, but others have not.

Red Flag Situation

Situation: The Operating Agreement for an LLC does not specify how profits will be distributed among the managers. One of the three managers contributes $50,000 while the other two contribute $25,000 each. The first year the LLC realizes a net profit of $30,000 and the major contributor claims $15,000 of the profits based on the percentage of capital contribution.

Potential Problem: When the Operating Agreement is silent as to distribution of profits, most state statutes provide profits will be distributed equally regardless of a manager's capital contribution.

Going Global

1. Limited liability companies originated in Germany in 1892. Among the countries recognizing the LLC form of business are Brazil, Chile, Cuba, France, Italy, Mexico, and Turkey.

2. Countries recognizing the LLC have specific requirements for its formation. Most require the word "limited" in the company name.

3. Failure to strictly comply with the host country's legal requirements may result in losing the limited liability protection of the LLC.

Reducing Your Risks

1. Understand the statutory requirements for establishing an LLC in your state.

2. Make certain your business includes the words "Limited Liability Company" or "LLC" in its company name. All states require the name of the business to indicate it is an LLC.

3. For federal taxation purposes, an LLC can file as a sole proprietorship; a Subchapter C or Subchapter S corporation; or a partnership. The choice is indicated by checking the appropriate "box" on IRS Form 8832. Make certain your LLC checks the appropriate box for the income tax classification it chooses to follow.

4. Consult with your accountant/financial advisor if necessary before determining the most appropriate income tax classification for your LLC.

5. If your LLC plans to conduct business in another state, make certain you are in compliance with the host state's LLC requirements for foreign (out-of-state) LLCs.

Sources of Information

1. Information on state laws regarding limited liability companies is available from Cornell at *http://www.law.cornell.edu/topics/state_statutes.html*. After accessing the site, type in "limited liability company."

2. Additional information is available at *http://www.law.uc.edu/LLC*.

3. Also visit *http://www.swlearning.com/blaw/fundamentals/fundamentals6e/fundamentals6e.html*. Go to "Interactive Study Center" and click on Chapter 24, "Sole Proprietorships, Partnerships, and Limited Liability Companies and Partnerships."

Limited Liability Partnership

(For additional information, *see Partnership.*)

The term *limited liability partnership (LLP)* refers to a hybrid form of business organization that combines certain aspects of the corporate form of business with those of a partnership. The LLP is usually utilized by professionals (such as attorneys, physicians, architects, and accountants) and by family-owned businesses, especially family-owned farms. The latter entity is referred to as a *Family Limited Partnership*. The LLP is based on state statutes and therefore its formation must conform to the laws of the state in which it is formed. Texas was the first state to adopt the LLP form of business organization.

Advantages of the LLP: In many states, a major advantage of the LLP is the limited liability of those partners who were not involved in the action that lead to a plaintiff's claim. This is in contrast to a general *partnership* where all of the general partners face *joint and several liability* for torts committed by another partner. Another advantage of the LLP involves taxation. The LLP allows the individual partners to pass through the business expenses and deductions to their own individual income taxes.

Red Flag Situation

Situation: An accounting firm operates as an LLP. One of the junior accountants/partners is sued for negligence (malpractice) by a client. The plaintiff also names the senior accountant who was responsible for supervising the junior accountant's work.

Potential Problem: According to partnership law, a supervising partner is also liable for the negligence of the partner involved in malpractice. Some states recognize the concept of proportionate liability based on the degree of each partners' negligence while other states do not and apply the concept of joint and several liability.

Disadvantages of the LLP: As mentioned previously, an LLP's existence is based on state statute. It must therefore comply with the statutory requirements of the state in which it is formed. These requirements include filing the appropriate papers with the designated state office (usually the Secretary of State). The business must also include either "Limited Liability Partnership" or "LLP" in its name.

Red Flag Situation

Situation: A company offering professional architectural services forms an LLP in one state. The company decides to expand its operations and opens an office in a neighboring state.

Potential Problem: An LLP formed in one state may not be recognized in another. Some states do not recognize the existence of a foreign LLP (an LLP formed in another state). Assuming a state does recognize foreign LLPs, that state may apply its own laws regarding LLPs in the case of a suit brought in the second state.

Family Limited Liability Partnership (FLLP): This form of LLP is frequently used by family farming operations. State statutes regulating FLLPs require a majority of the partners be members of the same family or a fiduciary agent acting for a family member. Some agricultural states provide specific advantages for this entity, including exemption from state transfer taxes when the partners in an FLLP transfer partnership real property from one to the other.

Going Global

Laws establishing the various forms of business organizations vary greatly throughout the world. Many countries do not yet recognize the LLP form of business organization.

Reducing Your Risks

1. Keep in mind that LLP laws are not consistent throughout the states. Seek legal and financial advice before determining whether the LLP form is best for you and your partners. Consider the tax and legal consequences of this form.

2. If you choose the LLP form, recognize that in order to enjoy the limited liability the form affords, you must comply strictly with state statutes.

3. Before expanding your LLP into another state, confirm that the second state will recognize a foreign LLP.

Sources of Information

1. The Small Business Administration discusses partnerships at *http://www.sba.gov/ starting/indexlaws.html*.

2. To learn more, go to *http://www.swlearning.com/blaw/fundamentals/ fundamentals6e/fundamentals6e.html*. Go to "Interactive Study Center" and click on Chapter 24, "Sole Proprietorships, Partnerships, and Limited Liability Companies and Partnerships."

Limited Partnership

(For additional information, *see Partnership*.)

The term *limited partnership* refers to a form of business organization comprised of at least one general partner and one or more limited partners. Both general and limited partnerships require: (1) an association of two or more persons; (2) to carry on a business as co-owners; and (3) for profit. In a limited partnership, the general partner faces unlimited personal liability for claims against the partnership while a limited partner's liability is generally limited to the amount of the limited partner's capital contribution. Limited partnerships are governed by state statutes. A majority of the states have adopted the Revised Uniform Limited Partnership Act (RULPA) in order to assure a certain degree of consistency regarding limited partnerships among the states. The RULPA requires the limited partnership file a Certificate of Limited Partnership with the appropriate state office.

Advantages of the Limited Partnership: A major advantage is the limited liability provided for the limited partners. In addition, the partners can pass through the partnership expenses as deductions on their individual taxes.

Disadvantages: A limited partnership is a statutory form of business and therefore a written certificate of Limited Partnership must be filed with the appropriate state office. Other formal statutory requirements must be met.

Red Flag Situation

Situation: A limited partner in a major retail company becomes dissatisfied with certain company policies and begins to actively participate in the management of the company.

Potential Problem: A limited partner who begins to actively participate in the management of the company runs the risk of losing the limited liability afforded to such a partner and may then be treated as a general partner and face unlimited personal liability.

How the RULPA May Fill in the Blanks: As a general rule, the provisions in the Certificate of Limited Partnership govern the operation of the business. If the Certificate is silent on certain matters, the provisions of the RULPA may apply. The following examples show how the RULPA fills in the blank.

1. If the Certificate does not designate how profits and losses will be shared, the RULPA provides they will be shared according to each partner's capital contribution.

2. If the Certificate does not designate how much authority each general partner will have in the management, the RULPA provides every general partner will have an equal voice.

RULPA's Order of Distribution of Assets Upon Liquidation: Upon the liquidation of a limited partnership, the assets (if any) are distributed in the following order:

1. Outside creditors and partner creditors.

2. Partners and former partners who were entitled to their distributions prior to their withdrawal according to the Certificate of the RULPA.

3. Partners in accordance with their capital contributions.

4. Partners according to profits.

Going Global

Partnership laws vary greatly in other countries. Some countries do not recognize the limited partnership as a form of business organization.

Reducing Your Risks

1. Seek legal and financial advice prior to establishing or joining a limited partnership. Make certain this form of organization fits into your own financial needs.

2. If you are a limited partner, avoid actively participating in management; otherwise you may lose the limited liability protection.

3. Recognize the risks involved in investing in a limited partnership. According to the rules of distribution, partners are third in line to recover their capital contributions.

Sources of Information

1. Information on the various forms of business organizations is available from the Small Business Administration at *http://www.sba.gov*. Click on "Staring Your Business."

2. More information on limited partnerships is available at *http://www.swlearning.blaw/fundamentals/fundamentals6e/fundamentals6e.html*. Go to "Interactive Study Center" and click on Chapter 24, "Sole Proprietorships, Partnerships, and Limited Liability Companies and Partnerships."

Mm

Mail and Wire Fraud

(For additional information, *see Fraud.*)

The terms *mail fraud* refers to the use of interstate mail to commit fraud in violation of federal criminal laws. The term *wire fraud* refers to the use of interstate television, radio or wire transmissions to commit fraud in violation of federal criminal laws.

Mail Fraud: The Mail Fraud Act of 1990 (18 U.S.C. §§ 1341-42) provides it is a federal crime to devise or intend to devise a scheme to defraud the public by using the mail or an interstate carrier. If the violation affects a financial institution, the defendant faces up to $1 million in fines and 30 years in prison.

Red Flag Situation

Situation: A real estate developer mails advertisements to thousands of individuals offering home sites for sale in the Southwest. The ads claim the sites are easily accessible when the developer knows there are no means of ingress and egress to the property. The developer considers the claims to be sales talk or "puffing." *Potential Problem:* The developer can be criminally liable under the Mail Fraud Act of 1990.

Wire Fraud: The Wire Fraud Act (18 U.S.C. § 1343) provides it is a federal crime to use the interstate wires, radio or television to devise or intend to devise a scheme to defraud. Individual violators face a fine plus up to 20 years in federal prison. If the fraud affects a financial institution, sanctions include fines up to $1 million and up to 30 years in federal prison.

Wire fraud can also be committed by using a fax machine or a computer (including e-mail communications). In one case, the Federal Trade Commission (FTC) charged an individual with wire fraud based on the defendant's auctioning off computers over the Internet, collecting the funds, and never delivering the items to the purchasers.

Going Global

Mail and wire fraud are considered serious offenses in many countries. Sanctions imposed may be much heavier than those imposed in the U.S.

Reducing Your Risks

1. Review any claims your business makes regarding the efficacy of its goods or services. False claims sent through the mail or by wire (including over fax machines and the Internet) can result in criminal liability if they are determined to be fraudulent.

2. Make certain those involved in marketing recognize the need to be able to substantiate any claims made about the goods or services your company offers to the public.

Sources of Information

1. To learn more about federal crimes, go to the Department of Justice site at *http://www.doj.gov*.

2. The Federal Trade Commission offers information on wire fraud at *http://www.ftc.gov*.

3. Also go to *http://www.swlearning.com/blaw/fundamentals/fundamentals6e/ fundamentals6e.html*. Go to "Court Case Updates" and click on "Criminal Law."

Mailbox Rule

(For additional information, *see* **Contracts**.)

The **mailbox rule**, also called the dispatch rule, refers to a rule in contract law providing that an acceptance to an offer is effective when the party accepting the offer (the offeree) drops the letter of acceptance in the mailbox or delivers the letter to a courier service. This rule applies when the offeree is using an authorized means of acceptance and the offeror did not stipulate that the acceptance would not be effective until actually received by the offeror. A means of acceptance (such as mail) is expressly authorized when the offeror designates the means and is implied authorized when the means is the same as that used by the offeror or any other reasonable means.

Example: Assume an electronics manufacturer writes to a retailer offering to sell 5,000 television sets at a specific price. The retailer's acceptance is effective as soon as the retailer drops the letter in the mailbox even if the manufacturer never receives the acceptance. To avoid this situation, the offeror may stipulate that the acceptance is not effective until it is actually received by the offeror.

Red Flag Situation

1. *Situation:* The owner of a commercial building writes to a prospective buyer, offering to sell the building for a specific price. The buyer drops the letter of acceptance into a mailbox outside the post office. The box is destroyed in a storm and the seller never receives the acceptance. Assuming the offeree is not interested, the property owner sells to another party.

   Potential Problem: A contract was formed when the buyer put his letter of acceptance in the mailbox. The first buyer can therefore sue for breach of contract.

Going Global

1. Contract laws vary throughout the world. Many countries do not recognize the mailbox rule.

2. The United Nations-sponsored Convention on the International Sale of Goods (CISG) does not recognize the mailbox rule. The CISG applies to the international sale of commercial goods between two parties whose places of business are in different countries and both of the countries are signatories to the convention. The parties have the right to "opt out" of the CISG.

Reducing Your Risks

1. To assure that you know whether the offeree has accepted your offer, consider providing in your offer that the acceptance will not be effective until you receive it.

2. If you are the offeree, be sure you can prove the time of your acceptance. For example, you may send the acceptance by certified mail. Keep a copy of your acceptance in case the original is lost in the mail or lost by the courier service.

Sources of Information

1. More information on contract law is available from *http://www.law.cornell.edu/topics/contracts.html*.

2. Also go to *http://www.swlearning.com/blaw/fundamentals/fundamentals6e/fundamentals6e.html*. Go to "Interactive Study Center" and click on Chapter 8, "Agreement and Consideration."

Mechanic's Lien

(For additional information, *see Liens*.)

The term *mechanic's lien* refers to a statutory lien available to a party who provides goods, labor or services relative to the purchase or improvement of real property. If the debtor fails to pay for the goods, labor or services, the lien holder can seek a foreclosure on the property. The property is then sold and the lien holder is paid from the proceeds of the sale. State statutes require the liens must be filed within a certain period after the goods or work is provided.

Red Flag Situation

Situation: A security company installs an expensive security system in a commercial building. The company files a mechanic's lien within the required time frame. The accountant for the property owner fails to pay the security company. *Potential Problem:* The creditor, after proper notice to the property owner, can have the building foreclosed upon and collect the amount due from the sales proceeds.

Going Global

Many countries recognize some form of the mechanic's lien for those who provide goods, services or labor for real property.

Reducing Your Risks

1. If your company provides goods, services or labor for property on credit, make certain a mechanic's lien is filed in a timely manner.

2. If you are a property owner utilizing a construction company, make certain that your prime contractor pays the subcontractors on time. When a property owner pays a prime contractor but the prime contractor does not pay a subcontractor, the property owner may be liable to the latter. An unpaid subcontractor who properly filed a mechanic's lien may force a foreclosure on the property even if the property owner paid the prime contractor.

3. Understand that expensive property can be subject to a foreclosure sale based on a mechanic's lien even if the amount of the lien is a very small percentage of the total value of the real property. The lien holder will be paid off and the remainder of the proceeds can go to the property owner (or the party holding the mortgage on the property).

Sources of Information

1. More information on liens is available from Cornell at *http://www.law.cornell.edu/ topics/debtor_creditor.html*.

2. Also go to *http://www.swlearning.com/blaw/fundamentals/fundamentals6e/ fundamentals6e.html*. Go to "Internet Applications" and click on Chapter 21, "Creditors' Rights and Bankruptcy."

Merchantability

(For additional information, *see Implied Warranties* and *Sales*.)

The term *merchantability* refers to an implied warranty that accompanies the sale or lease of goods (tangible, moveable property) when the seller is a merchant. Article 2 of the Uniform Commercial Code (UCC) applies to the sale of goods and Article 2A applies to the lease of goods. All of the states have adopted some form of the UCC. A complete discussion of merchantability is included in *Implied Warranties*.

Nn

Negligence

(For additional information, *see Agency*, *Product Liability* and *Torts.*)

The tort of ***negligence*** occurs when the defendant unintentionally breaches a duty owed to the plaintiff and injury results. Negligence cases include malpractice claims brought against professionals such as attorneys, accountants and financial advisors.

Elements of Negligence

The plaintiff must prove the following four elements in order to prevail in a negligence case:

1. the defendant owed a duty to the plaintiff;

2. the defendant breached that duty;

3. the breach of the duty was the actual and proximate (foreseeable) cause (of); and

4. plaintiff's injuries or damages.

Assume a client sues an accountant for malpractice in conducting an audit. The client must prove:

a. The accountant owed a duty to the client to perform the audit in a prudent manner as established by certain standards of the accounting profession. These standards are found in the Generally Accepted Accounting Principles (GAAP) and the General Accepted Auditing Standards (GAAS).

b. The accountant breached that duty by failing to perform in accordance with GAAS and therefore did not detect easily detectable fraud.

c. Failure to perform the audit according to GAAS was the actual and foreseeable cause.

d. Of the monetary damages plaintiff suffered.

The Causation Factor: One of the plaintiff's heaviest burdens in a negligence claim is meeting the foreseeability requirement. Assume a consulting firm's courier is delivering a document to a client across town during a snowstorm. The courier does not slow down but is driving within the regular speed limit. The car slides on the slick street and rams into an electric pole, causing an immediate outage that knocks out a brokerage firm's entire computer system for four hours. As a result, the brokerage firm suffers a huge financial loss and sues the courier's employer for negligence. A major hurdle for the plaintiff is proving that it was foreseeable that the failure to slow down in the storm would result in plaintiff's monetary damages many blocks away. This determination is a fact determination a jury must decide.

Red Flag Situation

Situation: A bank places an outdoor ATM machine in a poorly lit parking area adjacent to the bank building. A customer is robbed and beaten while using the ATM late at night.

Potential Problem: The customer may successfully sue for negligence based on the bank's failure to provide adequate lighting if the customer can prove it was foreseeable that failure to provide proper lighting could result in the robbery and attack.

Defenses Available in Negligence Cases: Four defenses are available to parties sued for negligence:

1. ***Assumption of Risk:*** This defense is available when the defendant proves the plaintiff knowingly and willingly assumed the risk that resulted in injury. Assume an employee voluntarily gets into the car of a coworker, knowing the latter had too much to drink at an office party. Due to the drunken condition, the driver causes an auto accident. The injured passenger sues the driver for negligence. The defendant can successfully defend the suit because the plaintiff knowingly and willingly assumed the risk by getting into the car with a drunk driver.

2. ***Superseding Cause:*** An independent event that breaks the connection between defendant's negligence act and the injuries plaintiff suffers may relieve the defen-

dant of liability. Assume that a factory worker's arm is cut at work due to a coworker's negligence. While being transported to the hospital, the ambulance driver runs a light and the injured factory worker sustains a severe head injury from the wreck that results. The coworker (and the coworker's employer) are liable for the arm injury but not for the head injury.

3. *Contributory Negligence:* In those states that recognize the defense of contributory negligence, the defendant is relieved of all liability if the plaintiff's own negligence contributed at all to the injury. The plaintiff may still recover however if the defendant had a "last clear chance" to avoid injuring the plaintiff.

4. *Comparative Negligence:* A majority of states recognize the defense of comparative negligence (rather than contributory negligence). This defense allows the plaintiff to recover even if plaintiff's own negligence contributed to the injury. The damages plaintiff receives will be based on the degree of negligence on defendant's part compared to the plaintiff's own degree of negligence.

Special Negligence Doctrines

1. *Res ipsa loquitur:* This term comes from the Latin phrase meaning "the facts speak for themselves." The doctrine is applied when the object or event that resulted in plaintiff's injuries was under the complete control of the defendant. Assume an airline crashes and there are no survivors or witness. The victims' families may sue the airline claiming this doctrine. The doctrine creates the rebuttable presumption that the defendant was negligent. The burden is then on the airline to prove the crash was not due to its negligence but to some other factor.

2. *Negligence per se:* This doctrine, meaning "negligence in itself," is useful when the plaintiff may not meet the foreseeable causation requirement. In order for the doctrine to apply, plaintiff must show:

a. the defendant breached a specific criminal statute (written law);

b. the statute is on the books to protect certain groups of persons from particular types of injuries; and

c. plaintiff is the group to be protected from the type of injury plaintiff suffered.

Assume a store clerk fails to obtain proper identification when selling a firearm. The purchaser was a convicted felon who should not own a gun. The purchaser takes the gun and holds up a bank in a neighboring town, shooting a bank guard. The seriously injured guard sues the store for selling the gun to a convicted felon. The plaintiff claims negligence per se applies. The plaintiff will win because (a) the retailer breached a statute requiring proper identification before selling a firearm; (b) the statute is to protect the public from being shot by convicted felons; and (c) the bank guard is in the group protected from the type of injury the guard suffered.

Special Negligence Statutes

1. Dram Shop Statute: A state dram shop statute holds that bartenders and tavern owners are negligent when injuries result from serving so many drinks that a customer becomes drunk in the establishment or by serving drinks to someone who is already drunk.

2. Social Host Statutes: In some states, individuals or businesses that host parties can be held liable when a guest becomes intoxicated and causes injuries either to the guest or to others. Courts have imposed social host liability for "bring your own bottle" parties where the guests provided their own alcohol.

Red Flag Situation

Situation: An employer hosts an annual holiday party. An employee drinks too much and causes a serious car accident while driving home.

Potential Problem: In many states, the employer can be liable based on hosting the party where the employee had too much to drink.

Going Global

1. Liability based on breach of duty is recognized throughout the world. In many civil law countries, this tort liability is found under the codal articles discussing "Obligations."

2. Many countries hold the employer liable for the tort (including negligence) committed by the employer "within the scope of employment."

Reducing Your Risks

1. Understand that an employer can be liable for the negligence of an employee committed "within the scope of employment."

2. Exercise care in the hiring of new employees. If a company fails to adequately check an applicant's background before hiring an employee and the employee later causes harm to the company or to others, the shareholders or other injured parties may sue for "negligence in hiring."

3. Make certain your employees comply with statutes applicable to transactions with the public, such as requiring proper identification before selling certain items, in order to avoid liability based on negligence per se.

4. Recognize the potential liability associated with serving alcohol at job-related parties. The employer may face liability for injuries resulting from the negligent acts of a guest who drinks too much at the party.

Sources of Information

1. Information on negligence is available at *http://www.swlearning.com/blaw/ fundamentals/fundamnetals6e/fundamentals6e.html*. Go to "Court Case Updates" and click on "Torts."

2. Articles on negligence are available at *http://www.lawguru.com/ilawlib*. Go to "Laws of all jurisdictions" (arranged by subject) and click on "Tort Law."

Negotiable Instruments

(For additional information, *see Holder in Due Course.*)

A *negotiable instrument* is a form of commercial paper that may afford the holder of the instrument better rights than those held by the party transferring the paper. The requirements for a negotiable instrument are specified in Articles 3 and 4 of the Uniform Commercial Code (UCC).

Purposes: A negotiable instrument serves two purposes:

1. It may be a substitute for money (i.e., a check) and

2. It may be a credit device (i.e., a promissory note).

Requirements: In order for a commercial paper to qualify as a negotiable instrument, it must meet the following requirements:

1. It is in writing. The writing must be permanent and portable (moveable in commerce).

2. The instrument is signed by the maker (promise paper) or the drawer (order paper). The signature does not have to be a full "wet" signature. For example, it may be made electronically or may be in the form of an "X."

3. The instrument contains an unconditional promise or order to pay.

4. Payment is in a sum certain of money. The money can be in any recognized currency.

5. The instrument is payable either on demand or at a specified time.

6. The instrument is payable either to the order of a party or to bearer. (Checks are an exception to this requirement.)

Types of Negotiable Instruments

1. Order instrument: An order instrument consists of three parties. The drawer

orders the *drawee* to pay the *payee*. Examples include checks and trade acceptances.

2. Promise instrument: In a promise instrument, the maker promises to pay the payee. Examples include promissory notes and certificates of deposit issued by a bank.

Importance of Making Certain an Instrument is Negotiable: When a negotiable instrument is held by a party who qualifies as a ***holder in due course (HDC)***, it is possible for the HDC to obtain better rights to the instrument than those held by the transferring party.

Red Flag Situations

1. ***Situation:*** A financial servicing company purchases a promissory note from a farm equipment company. In the note, a farmer agreed to pay $75,000 for a large tractor to be used in the farming operations. The note included a provision that annual payments were due "upon the harvest of my wheat crops each year." Due to mechanical problems with the equipment, the farmer refused to continue payments.
   Potential Problem: The note does not qualify as a negotiable instrument and therefore the new holder cannot be a Holder in Due Course. As a mere holder (rather than a HDC), any defenses the maker can raise against paying the original payee are also valid defenses for not paying the holder. The note is not negotiable because (1) payment is conditional upon a crop being harvested each year and (2) the instrument is not payable either on demand or at a definite time.

2. ***Situation:*** A finance company purchases a trade acceptance from Reid Manufacturing Company. The instrument reads, "Pay to Reid Manufacturing Co."
   Potential Problem: The instrument is not a negotiable instrument and therefore the current holder cannot be a HDC. The instrument is not negotiable because it is not payable to order or to bearer. It should have read, "Pay to the Order of Reid Manufacturing Co."

3. ***Situation:*** A property owner sells a commercial building. The buyer executes a promissory note to the seller, which the latter plans to sell in order to get immediate cash. The note states it is "Subject to the terms of the mortgage on this property."
   Potential Problem: The note does not qualify as a negotiable instrument. The note is subject to the terms stated in a separate document (the mortgage) and therefore is not an unconditional promise to pay.

Going Global

1. Negotiable instruments play a key role in international commerce. Requirements for negotiability are different in different countries.

2. In the United Kingdom and many other countries, the term "Bill of Exchange" is used for the instrument described as a "draft" in the U.S.

3. Negotiable drafts (bills of exchange) are used extensively in international sales transactions.

Reducing Your Risks

1. When accepting an instrument from a debtor, make certain it meets all the requirements to qualify as a negotiable instrument; otherwise, neither you nor future holders can qualify as a HDC.

2. If your company purchases commercial paper from other creditors, confirm that the paper meets all requirements for a negotiable instrument in order for your company to qualify as a HDC.

Sources of Information

1. An overview of negotiable instruments law is available at *http://www.swlearning.com/blaw/fundamentals/fundamentals6e/fundamentals6e.html*. Go to "Interactive Study Center" and click on Chapter 18, "Negotiability, Transferability and Liability."

2. For more information, go to *http://www.law.cornell.edu/topics/negotiability.html*.

Oo

Occupational Safety and Health Act

The federal *Occupational Safety and Health Act* of 1970 (the Act) requires employers to provide healthful and safe working conditions for employees (29 U.S.C. §§ 553, 651-678). The agency responsible for setting standards and enforcing the Act is the Occupational Safety and Health Administration (OSHA). A division of the Department of Labor, OSHA has the right to obtain a warrant to inspect facilities subject to the Act.

Employers' Duties Under the Act: The following are examples of duties mandated by OSHA:

1. Employers who hire at least eleven employees must maintain records of all occupational injuries and illnesses.

2. In addition, all employers subject to the Act must file a report regarding any job-related illness or accident. Notification must occur within 48 hours when a death results or at least five injured employees require hospitalization.

3. OSHA requires employers comply with OSHA standards and regulations pertaining to the employer's types of business or the comparable state standards.

4. The employer must display the OSHA Safe and Healthful Workplaces poster (or the state equivalent) in a place easily visible for employees and prospective employees.

The poster contains information relevant to rights and responsibilities under the Act.

5. Employers must inform workers of hazardous chemicals in the workplace and provide training regarding the safe handling of those chemicals.

Red Flag Situation

Situation: An accounting firm employs 50 employees in the office building the firm owns. Ten workers are rushed to the hospital complaining of severe respiratory distress one morning. The firm fails to report the incident to OSHA within 48 hours.

Potential Problem: The employer violated the reporting requirements of OSHA and is therefore subject to fines. If it determined the violation was willful, criminal sanctions may also be imposed.

Going Global

Laws regulating the work environment vary greatly throughout the world. Companies establishing a work place abroad need to become familiar with regulations in the host country.

Reducing Your Risks

1. Understand that in addition to OSHA, the workplace environment is subject to applicable state laws. If your company is covered by a state agency that administers a safety and health plan approved by OSHA, you may be subject to state inspections.

2. If you have employees who conduct their work in their homes, become familiar with OSHA's requirements regarding at-home work sites. If the employer provides dangerous materials or work processes which the employee uses at home, the employer can be liable for resulting injuries or illnesses.

3. Understand that OSHA's reporting and audit requirements may include remote work sites (such as vehicles and airports) in the future. It is therefore important to monitor the latest OSHA regulations for new provisions.

Sources of Information

1. To learn more about OSHA regulations, visit *http://www.osha.gov*. Go to "Frequently Asked Questions–General OSHA."

2. More information is available at *http://www.swlearning.com/blaw/fundamentals/fundamentals6e/fundamentals6e.html*. Go to "Court Case Updates" and click on "Employment Law."

$$Pp$$

Partnership

(For additional information, *see* **Agency, Limited Partnership** and **Limited Liability Partnership.**)

According to the Uniform Partnership Act (UPA), a general **partnership** is defined as "an association of two or more persons to carry on as co-owners a business for profit." (UPA § 6(1)). Currently all of the states except Louisiana have adopted either the UPA or the Revised Uniform Partnership Act (RUPA).

Determining the Existence of a Partnership: Disputes frequently arise over whether a partnership actually exists. In making the determination, a court will examine the business entity in light of the UPA definition. The sharing of profits and losses does not automatically create a partnership. For example, the UPA specifically provides the sharing of profits in the following situations does not in itself infer a partnership:

(a) as a debt by installments or otherwise;

(b) as wages to an employee or rent to a landlord;

(c) as an annuity to a widow or representative of a deceased partner;

(d) as interest on a loan, though the amount of payments vary with the profits of the business; and

(e) as the consideration for the sale of a good-will of a business or the property by installments or otherwise. (UPA Section 7 (4))

How the UPA Fills in the Blanks: A partnership agreement that is not covered by the ***Statute of Frauds*** (requiring certain contracts must be in writing to be enforceable) can be oral. The written agreement is referred to as the Articles of Partnership. If the partners do not specify certain terms in the written or verbal agreement, the UPA will "fill in the blanks" and determine those open terms. The following are examples of how the UPA fills in open terms:

1. Unless specified otherwise, all partners have equal rights in the management and conduct of the business. (UPA § 18e)

2. Each partner shall share equally in the profits and surplus. (UPA § 18a)

3. No person can become a partner without the unanimous consent of all the partners. (UPA § 18g)

Red Flag Situation

1. ***Situation:*** Three individuals enter into a partnership agreement to establish an advertising agency. Partner A contributes $100,000 in capital while B and C each contribute $10,000. The agreement is silent as to how profits will be distributed. The first year the agency realizes a profit of $60,000.
   Potential Problem: Despite the fact that Partner A contributed ten times as much in capital as the other two, the UPA will "fill in the blanks" and each partner will receive $20,000 in profits.

2. ***Situation:*** In the advertising agency above, Partners B and C recommend a major change in management policy. The partnership agreement does not specify each partner's rights in the management of the business.
   Potential Problem: Partners B and C, despite their smaller contributions to capital, can control the management decisions because the UPA provides each partner will have an equal right in the management if the agreement is silent on the matter.

The Applicability of Agency Law to Partnerships: Agency law governs the relationship between a partner and the partnership. As an agent of the partnership (the partnership itself is the principal in the agency relationship), an individual partner can bind the partnership if the partner had express, implied or apparent authority. (Types of agent authority are further explained in the section on agency.)

Agency law also determines the duties a partner owes to the partnership, including the duty to notify the partnership of any knowledge the partner obtains that is relative to the partnership. This duty is based on the fact that any information the agent has relative to the business is imputed to the partnership entity. (A complete discussion of an agent's duties is discussed in the topic on agency.)

A Partner's Liability for Partnership Contracts and Debts: In a majority of states, partners are jointly liable for partnership contracts and debts. In this situation, a plaintiff suing the partnership lists all partners in the suit. According to the RUPA, each partner faces joint and several liability for debts (RUPA § 306); therefore, only one partner may face liability for the entire debt. The creditor may sue the other partners later.

A Partner's Liability for Partnership Torts: According to partnership law in every state, partners are jointly and severally liable for partnership torts. (UPA § 15a)

Red Flag Situation

Situation: Financial consultants A, B, and C form a general partnership. While B and C are out of town, A advises a client on a financial matter. The dissatisfied client decides to bring a malpractice (negligence) suit.

Potential Problem: Each of the three partners faces joint and several liability. As a result, B and/or C can be held liable for A's negligence.

Ending the Partnership: Two steps are involved in the termination of a partnership. The first step, dissolution, results when one or more partners cease association with the partnership. Any partner planning to withdraw must notify all other partners. In addition, the business must notify all third parties who may be affected. The second step is the winding up process, where partnership assets are collected and distributed.

Dissolution may occur based on the acts of the partners to dissolve the partnership. In addition, the partnership may automatically dissolve by operation of law when a partner dies, or becomes bankrupt or when the partnership operations become illegal.

How Assets Are Distributed When a Partnership Ends: According to the UPA, partnership assets are distributed as follows:

(1) Those owing to creditors other than partners.

(2) Those owing to partners other than for capital and profits.

(3) Those owing to partners in respect of capital.

(4) Those owing to partners in respect of profits. (UPA § 40b)

The RUPA places partner creditors along with outside creditors in the first rank to be paid. In determining a partner's share in the assets or liabilities, the RUPA combines the partner's capital contribution and share of profits and losses (RUPA § 808).

How Liabilities Are Paid: According to the UPA, when liabilities exceed assets, partners are liable for debts in accordance with the agreement. If the agreement is silent, the UPA "fills in the blanks" and provides partners shall contribute to losses according to their share in the profits. (UPA § 18a) If one or more partners are insolvent or refuses to contribute, "...the other partners shall contribute their share to the liabilities, and in the relative proportion in which they share the profits, the additional amount necessary to pay the liabilities." (UPA § 40d)

Going Global

Partnership laws vary greatly in other countries. Many countries require a written agreement.

Reducing Your Risks

1. In order to assure all partners understand the terms of the partnership, insist on written Articles of Partnership.

2. Have your own attorney review the Articles before signing to make certain the provisions are in your best interest.

3. Understand the potential personal liability you face in a general partnership.

4. Make certain the other partners are responsible and solvent.

5. Consider the limited liability offered in a limited liability partnership when adopting a form of business entity.

Sources of Information:

1. Information on partnerships is available at *http://www.law.cornell.edu/topics/partnership.html*.

2. To learn more, go to *http://www.swlearning.com/blaw/fundamentals/fundamentals6e/fundamentals6e.html*. Go to "Interactive Study Center" and click on Chapter 24, "Sole Proprietorships, Partnerships and Limited Liability Corporations and Partnerships."

Patents

(For additional information, *see Copyrights, Intellectual Property Rights, Trade Secrets.*)

The grant from the U.S. government providing an inventor the exclusive right to an invention or design for a specified period of time is referred to as a patent. The U.S. Constitution grants Congress the power "To promote the Progress of Science and useful Arts, by securing for limited Times to Authors and Inventors the exclusive Right to their respective Writings and Discoveries." (Article I, § 8)

Subject Matter for Patent Protection: There are basically three categories of patents:

1. Utility patents apply to inventions as well as discoveries. Examples include computer hardware and genetically modified animals. Processes are also included in this category. Recently a patent was awarded for a "one-click" order system for Internet users.

2. Design patents apply to ornamental designs for goods.

3. Plant patents protect varieties of plants such as freeze-resistant citrus fruit.

In addition, the U.S. Supreme Court has held that business processes can be protected by patents.

Duration of Patents: Patents for inventions are valid for 20 years; design patents are valid for 14 years. A patent holder has the exclusive right to make, use and sell the subject matter of the patent for the designated time.

Obtaining a Patent: Patent applications are filed with the U.S. Patent and Trademark Office. In order to obtain a patent, the applicant must show that the subject matter is novel, genuine, useful, and not obvious.

Red Flag Situation

Situation: A soft drink company develops the formula for a new low-calorie, vitamin-enriched beverage. The company immediately applies for a patent. ***Potential Problem:*** Due to online patent databases, the formula is readily attainable worldwide via the Internet. Both the U.S. Patent and Trademark Office and the European Patent Office provide their databases online via the Internet. Frequently inventors decide to protect the invention as a trade secret in order to avoid the worldwide publication.

Going Global

1. In many countries, patent protection is awarded to the first party to file an application. In the U.S., the patent is awarded to the first party to invent.

2. The international Trade-Related Aspects of Intellectual Property Rights (TRIPS) Agreement addresses intellectual property protection in the signatory countries. TRIPS is now part of the World Trade Organization (WTO) agreement. WTO member countries must provide foreign patent holders with the same rights afforded domestic patent holders.

Reducing Your Risks

1. If your company decides to apply for a patent, make certain that only those parties who are critical to the application process see the design or formula.

2. Seek legal counsel with expertise in the area of patent law. Patents are frequently denied based on the failure to provide all necessary information in the application.

3. If you obtain a patent, be prepared to monitor for patent infringement both domestically and internationally. Patent infringements cost U.S. companies billions of dollars annually.

Sources of Information

1. Extensive information is available from the U.S. Patent and Trademark Office at *http://www.uspto.gov*.

2. Information on international patents is available from Cornell University at *http://www.law.cornell.edu/topics/patents.html*.

3. For more information, visit *http://www.swlearning.com/blaw/fundamentals/ fundamentals6e/fundamentals6e.html*. Go to "Court Case Updates" and click on "Intellectual Property."

Product Liability

(For additional information, *see Contracts, Express Warranties, Implied Warranties, Fraud, Negligence, Sales, Strict Liability* and *Torts*.)

Product liability refers to the liability the manufacturer or seller of goods faces when a party alleges injuries resulting from those goods. The plaintiff's claim may be based on misrepresentation, fraud, breach of warranty, negligence, or strict liability.

When the Plaintiff Alleges Misrepresentation or Fraud: The buyer may sue based on the intentional torts of misrepresentation or fraud. Assume a retailer assures a customer that a computer keyboard is ergonomically safe. The customer develops carpal tunnel syndrome and then learns the keyboard is improperly designed. The customer sues the retailer, who was unaware of the flaw. To prevail in a claim of misrepresentation, the customer must prove the following:

1. The defendant misrepresented a material fact in order to induce the buyer to rely on the statement.

2. The plaintiff relied on the statement.

3. The reliance was reasonable.

4. The defendant knew the statement was false and intentionally mislead the plaintiff.

Claim Based on Breach of Warranty: The sale of goods may carry with it certain express or implied warranties.

Express Warranties (*see also* ***Express Warranties***): According to Article 2 of the Uniform Commercial Code (UCC), the seller of goods may create an express warranty by: (1) making a factual assertion; (2) through a description of the goods; or (3) by showing a sample of the goods.

Implied Warranties (*see also* ***Implied Warranties***): Among the implied warranties that accompany the sale of goods are the implied warranties of merchantability and fitness for a particular purpose.

The implied warranty of merchantability applies only to sellers who are merchants. According to Article 2, merchantable goods are "reasonably fit for the ordinary purposes for which such goods are used."

The implied warranty of fitness for a particular purpose applies when the seller knows the buyer's specific needs and knows the buyer is relying on the seller to select the goods.

Claims Based on Negligence: A person injured by a product may successfully sue for negligence providing the plaintiff can prove the four essential elements of negligence:

1. the defendant owed a duty to plaintiff;

2. defendant breached that duty;

3. the breach was the actual and proximate (foreseeable) cause; and

4. of plaintiff's injuries.

The plaintiff does not have to be the purchaser of the goods. For example, a driver is injured due to a defective tire on an approaching truck. Due to the defective tire, the truck driver loses control and hits the oncoming car. The injured auto driver may sue the tire manufacturer for negligence. (The plaintiff may also sue based on strict liability.)

Claim Based on Strict Product Liability: The tort doctrine of strict liability is applied in two situations: (1) when the defendant is engaged in an ultra hazardous activity and (2) when a plaintiff is injured by a product that is considered unreasonably dangerous.

Potential Defendants in Strict Product Liability Claims: The defendant must be in the business of selling or leasing goods. The manufacturer, seller (retailer and wholesaler), distributor, and lessor of the defective products all face potential product liability.

Requirements for Strict Product Liability: In order to prevail, the plaintiff must prove (1) the product was defective when it left the defendant; (2) the product was not substantially changed from the time of sale until the injury; (3) the defect was the proximate (foreseeable) cause of physical or property damage to plaintiff; and (4) most states also require that the defect rendered the product unreasonably dangerous.

Defects may occur in the manufacture, design or provision of warnings regarding the product.

Red Flag Situations

1. *Situation:* The manufacturer of a grass edger does not insert a warning advising users of the risk of removing the safety shield. A customer removes the shield and suffers an eye injury.
   Potential Problem: The manufacturer had the duty to warn of the dangers resulting from misuse of the product if a court determines the misuse was foreseeable.

2. *Situation:* The injured party in the above example decides to sue the retailer rather than the manufacturer.
   Potential Problem: All parties in the distribution chain face potential liability. It does not matter that the retailer never opened the sealed box containing the product before it was sold to the plaintiff.

Defenses Available: To prevail, the plaintiff must meet the requirements for strict product liability listed above. The following additional defenses are available to the defendant: (1) assumption of risk; (2) misuse of the product; (3) comparative or contributory negligence; and (4) the injury was due to a "commonly known danger."

Going Global

Many countries recognize product liability today. The elements plaintiff must prove vary in different jurisdictions.

Reducing Your Risks

1. Understand that if your company is in the business of selling or leasing products, you face potential product liability even if the product arrived at your business sealed and was never altered.

2. Make certain that the manufacturer of the goods you lease or sell is a responsible party. In case you are sued for product liability, you will need to seek indemnification.

3. Carry adequate liability insurance in case you are sued for product liability.

Sources of Information

1. To learn more about product liability, visit *http://www.law.cornell.edu*. Go to "Law About" and "All Topics Alphabetically" and then click on "Product Liability."

2. For more information, visit *http://www.swlearning.com/blaw/fundamentals/fundamentals6e/fundamentals6e.html*. Go to "Interactive Study Center" and click on Chapter 17, "Warranties and Product Liability.

Property

(For additional information, see ***Bailments, Eminent Domain, Gift*** and ***Intellectual Property.***)

Property refers to those rights a person holds that can be protected and enforced by the law.

Categories of Property: Property may be categorized in several ways:

1. Tangible and Intangible
Tangible property has a physical existence and therefore can be touched and felt. Examples include computers, crops growing on trees, and cattle.
Intangible property has no physical existence of its own. Examples include patents, copyrights, and accounts receivable.

2. Real and Personal
Real property is tangible and includes the land, the surface below, the air above, and items attached to it (fixtures).
Personal property is movable property. It may be tangible (a desk) or intangible (a trademark).

Ways of Acquiring Real Property

1. By deed. A deed is required when real property is conveyed by purchase or gift. In order to be valid, the deed must meet the statutory requirements of the state in which the property is located. As a general rule, the deed must include the names of the grantor and grantee; words showing the grantor is conveying the property;

legal description, and the signature of the grantor. The deed is recorded in the proper governmental office.

2. By will or inheritance.

3. By eminent domain. The U. S. Constitution provides that a governmental entity can take private property for a public purpose if the owner is justly compensated. (For details, *see Eminent Domain*.)

4. By adverse possession. Property laws in every state permit another party to become the legal owner of real property by using the property without the owner's permission for a specified period of time and meeting other statutory requirements. Generally, adverse possession requires the following:

   a. possession of the property in continuous for the required time;

   b. possession is open for the world to see;

   c. possession is hostile (without the owner's permission); and

   d. the possessor is the only physical occupant of the property.

Red Flag Situation

Situation: A consulting firm owns a small office building. A retail store is constructed next door. The parking lot for the store encroaches on the firm's property by six feet without the owner's permission.

Potential problem: If the retail store continues to use the six feet for the required period of time, it may become the legal owner of that real property.

Fixtures: A fixture is a piece of property that was originally considered tangible personal (movable) property but is now considered real property. When determining whether property is now a fixture, a court will usually consider the following factors:

1. Whether the item is now permanently attached to the real property. For example, a slab of marble (personal property) that is installed in a new building as a fireplace mantel is now considered a fixture.

2. If the questioned property is intended to be permanently used with the real property. An example of a fixture is an automatic garage door opener.

Disputes over fixtures frequently arise in real estate transactions. Unless the parties agree to the contrary, the buyer becomes the owner of the land, the building, and the fixtures.

Red Flag Situation

Situation: The owner of a bank building contracts to sell the real estate. The seller plans to remove the ceiling fans, chandeliers, and drapes in the lobby and install them in a new bank. The sales contract does not exclude these items from the property to be sold.

Potential problem: If a dispute arises as to the owner of these items, a court will probably consider the items fixtures and conveyed with the sale of the building.

Ways of Acquiring Personal Property:

1. by possession (for additional information, see the discussion of lost and abandoned property below);

2. by purchase;

3. by gift (for more information *see Gifts*);

4. by accession or adding on additional parts;

5. by confusion or commingling fungible items;

6. by inheritance or will; and

7. by production or making an item.

Mislaid, Lost and Abandoned Personal Property

Mislaid Property: (For additional information, *see Bailment.*) Personal property is considered mislaid when the owner intentionally places the property in a certain place and then departs, inadvertently leaving the item behind. As a general rule, an involuntary bailment is created and the owner/lessor of the property where the item is left becomes the involuntary bailee. The bailee then has the duty to take reasonable care of the property until the owner reclaims it.

Red Flag Situation

Situation: A client visiting a stock brokerage firm places an expensive hand-held computer on the conference table. Later the client departs, inadvertently leaving the computer on the table. The stockbroker sees the computer but does not put it in a safe place. Later a third party steals the computer.

Potential problem: An involuntary bailment was created. Once a representative of the firm knew (or should have known) the computer was left on its premises, an involuntary bailment was created. The firm then had the duty to take reasonable care of the computer until the owner reclaimed it. By failing to take reasonable care, the firm is liable for the theft of the computer.

Lost Property: Personal property is lost when the owner unknowingly loses possession of it. The finder of lost property has better title to it than anyone except the true owner. A state's estray statute provides the finder of lost property may become the true owner after a specified period of time if the finder complies with all statutory requirements, including proper notification to the public that the property has been found.

Abandoned Property: Personal property is abandoned when the owner puts it in a certain place and intentionally walks away from the property. As a general rule, the finder of abandoned property can become the true owner if statutory requirements are met.

Going Global

1. Property laws vary greatly throughout the world, including the laws regarding fixtures.

2. In some countries, foreign investors cannot own more than 49 percent of real property.

3. In many countries, the government may take specific property owned by a foreigner. This taking is referred to as expropriation. The taking of the private property of a foreigner without compensations is referred to as confiscation. Governmental taking of an entire industry is referred to as nationalization.

4. Many foreign countries also recognize the right to become the legal owner of real property through adverse possession.

Reducing Your Risks

1. In selling real property, make certain the sales contract designates any fixtures you plan to take with you; otherwise, they are conveyed to the buyer.

2. If you are involved in a real estate transaction, confirm that the deed is valid according to state statute.

3. Before purchasing real property, review all building and zoning restrictions that may impact your future use of the property.

4. When purchasing a condominium or a unit in a cooperative building, understand that all owners are responsible for the maintenance of the common areas, such as the hallways, elevators, and surrounding landscape. Also determine whether a simple majority of the owners can vote for an improvement (such as a swimming pool) that all owners must pay for.

5. When purchasing commercial or residential property, condition your purchase on a satisfactory report by a licensed building inspector.

6. Require a satisfactory environmental assessment as a condition to your purchase of real property. If the building or land is later found to be contaminated, you as the current owner can be financially liable for the cleanup.

7. If you are associated with a nonprofit organization, understand that if real property donated to the organization is determined to be contaminated, the current owner (not the donor) is responsible for the cleanup.

8. If your company invests in real property abroad, consider the advantages of obtaining political risk insurance.

9. Insist upon the seller providing a title policy when you purchase real property.

10. Have your own legal counsel review any real estate documents prior to signing.

11. Make certain your company's real property has a current survey in order to avoid another party encroaching and becoming the new owner by adverse possession.

Sources of Information

1. To learn more about real property, go to *http://www.swlearning.com/blaw/fundamentals/fundamentals6e/fundamentals6e.html*. Go to "Interactive Study Guide" and click on Chapter 29, "Real Property."

2. Information about commercial property is available from the U.S. Department of Housing and Urban Development at *http://www.hud.gov*.

3. Political risk insurance is discussed at *http://www.opic.gov*.

Qq

Quasi Contract

(For additional information, *see **Contracts**.*)

The courts will hold that a fictional **quasi contract** (also referred to as an implied-in-law contract) exists when failure to do so would result in unjust enrichment for one of the parties.

Implied contracts: In contrast to an express contract, where the parties expressly agree to the contractual terms, an implied contract may exist in two situations:

1. Implied in fact contracts: The parties may imply through their actions (rather than through an express agreement) their intention to enter into a contract. Assume a software company takes its financial records to an accounting firm to prepare its annual tax returns. The client does not expressly agree to pay the firm a specified amount of amount. By their actions, the client has impliedly agreed to pay a reasonable fee and the firm has impliedly agreed to perform the audit in a timely and competent manner.

2. Implied in law or quasi contract A court will find that a quasi contract exists when the following requirements are met:

   a. plaintiff conveyed a benefit on the defendant;

   b. defendant knowingly and willing accepted the benefit; and

c. defendant knew that the plaintiff would not convey such a benefit without the expectation of some type of compensation.

Red Flag Situation

Situation: The director of the computer division of a bank requests that a computer service company repair the department's recently acquired computer. The repairperson misunderstands the work order and begins to service and repair all 30 computers in the department. The director, realizing the error, stands by and does nothing. When the service company sends a bill for work on all 30 computers, the director refuses to pay, claiming the bank expressly agreed to pay for service on only one piece of equipment.

Potential problem: A court will likely find a quasi contract exists because the director knowingly and willing accepted repair services on all 30 computers, knowing the service company would not do the work without expectation of compensation. Failure to pay for the services would result in unjust enrichment for the bank. (If the repair work was done over the weekend and the bank was unaware of the additional service and repair, the bank would not be liable because it did not knowingly and willing accept the additional benefits.)

Going Global

Many countries recognize the concept of a fictional quasi-contract and their courts will order the party who knowingly and willingly receives unrequested benefits to pay in order to avoid unjust enrichment.

Reducing Your Risks

1. Understand that your company may have to pay for benefits it knowingly and willing accepts event though it never expressly agreed to pay if a court determines the company would be unjustly enriched otherwise.

Sources of Information

1. Information on implied contracts is available at *http://www.swlearning.com/blaw/fundamentals/fundamentals6e/fundamentals6e.html*. Go to "Interactive Study Guide" and click on Chapter 7, "Nature and Classifications."

2. At the above Web site, go to "Court Case Updates" and click on "Contracts" for more information.

Ss

S Corporation

(For additional information, *see* ***Close Corporation*** and ***Corporation***.)

An ***S corporation*** is a hybrid form of business entity that combines certain aspect of the corporate form with those of a partnership. The S corporation offers the advantage of a corporation by providing limited liability for its shareholders. It resembles a partnership by allowing the entity's income and expenses to pass through to the shareholders. In certain situations, a close corporation can elect to be treated as an S corporation for tax purposes.

Requirements: In order to qualify as an S corporation, the federal Subchapter S Revision Act of 1982 requires the following:

1. The entity is a domestic corporation and none of the shareholders are nonresident aliens.

2. Shareholders do not include partnerships and certain types of trusts.

3. The total number of shareholders does not exceed 75.

4. Only one class of stock is offered.

5. The S corporation is not part of an affiliation of corporations.

Red Flag Situation

Situation: An entity operating as an S corporation determines it needs to attract additional capital investment and offers shares to new investors. The number of shareholders jumps to 85, including a nonresident alien.

Potential problem: An S corporation cannot have more than 75 shareholders and none can be a nonresident alien. The entity therefore no longer qualifies for S status.

Going Global

1. Corporation laws vary throughout the world. Some countries recognize a form similar to the S corporation.

2. Many countries do not allow foreign investors to own a controlling interest in a domestic corporation.

3. U. S. corporations are required to pay income tax on income earned from the corporation's foreign sources. Different rules apply to a foreign subsidiary of a U.S. corporation.

4. In many countries, the government must approve any foreign investment in a domestic corporation.

Reducing Your Risks

1. Seek competent legal and financial advice before determining if the S corporation offers the most advantages for your business.

2. Consider the benefits of other forms of business entities, including the limited liability company and the limited liability partnership and the additional flexibility each offers.

3. If your company selects the S form, make certain you comply with all requirements for maintaining the status.

Sources of Information

1. To learn more about corporate law in your state, visit *http://www.law.cornell.edu/topics/state_statutes.html*.

2. Additional information is available at *http://www.law.uc.edu/ccl*.

3. Information on corporation law in other countries is available from the World Trade Organization at *http://www.wto.org*.

4. Also go to *http://www.swlearning.com/blaw/fundamentals/fundamentals6e/fundamentals6e.html*. Go to "Interactive Study Guide" and click on Chapter 25,

"Corporate Formation, Financing, and Terminations."

Sales Law

(For additional information, *see **Contracts, Implied Warranties** and **Statute of Frauds**.*)

Sales law applies to the transfer of title to goods (tangible, movable property) from one party to another. Article 2 of the Uniform Commercial Code (UCC) governs these sales.

Article 2 and Mixed Contracts: Sometimes a contract will include the sale of both goods and services. In that case, Article 2 will generally apply if the predominant purpose of the sale involves goods. Assume a real estate firm purchases a new carpet. The price includes both the carpet and the installation. The buyer claims the carpet is inferior and the seller has breached Article 2's implied warranty of merchantability. The seller claims Article 2 does not apply because the contract includes the service of installing the carpet. In this situation, a court would likely determine the predominate purpose of the contract was the purchase of the carpet (goods) rather than the installation service. In that case, Article 2's implied warranty of merchantability would apply.

Article 2 and the Sale of Food and Beverages: Article 2 specifically provides that the sale of foods and beverages is considered a sale of goods regardless of whether they are consumed on the business premises (in a restaurant or bar) or consumed elsewhere.

How Article 2 Differs from the Common Law Contract Law

1. Open terms under Article 2: According to common law contract law (contract law), all essential terms must be included in order for the agreement to be enforceable. In contrast, a contract for the sale of goods can have open (blank) terms and Article 2 will fill in the blanks. Following are examples of how Article 2 can provide missing terms:

   a. Open price: If the parties do not specify a price, the price will be reasonable price at the time of delivery of the goods.

   b. Open delivery terms: If delivery terms are blank, delivery will occur at the seller's place of business. If seller has no place of business, delivery will be at seller's home or the location of the third party who is holding the goods.

   c. Open payment terms: If the parties do not agrees as to the medium of payment, the buyer can pay in any commercially acceptable manner, including check and credit card. If the seller demands cash at time of delivery, the seller must allow the buyer adequate time to obtain the cash.

2. Special rules on the offer: According to contract law, the offeror can revoke an offer any time before the offeree accepts with the exception of an option contract (where the offeree pays to keep the option to buy open). Article 2 recognizes the irrevocable firm offer. If the seller of goods is a merchant in the business of selling that type of goods and promises in a signed writing that the offer will remain open for a specified period of time, the merchant cannot revoke the offer during that time.

Red Flag Situation

Situation: A car dealer sends a signed letter to a corporate executive. The dealer offers to sell a new luxury car for a certain price. The letter states "This offer will remain open for 30 days." Ten days after the letter is sent a customer comes into the dealership and offers the seller $1,000 more for the same car. The dealer sells the car immediately. The following week the corporate executive comes in to accept the offer.

Potential problem: The executive can successfully sue the car dealer for breach of contract. The dealer made an irrevocable firm offer and therefore could not revoke the offer and sell the car to another party before the 30 days passed.

3. Special rules on acceptance: According to contract law, the acceptance must be the mirror image of the offer. If the offeree adds any new terms, the offeree has rejected the original offer and made a counteroffer. In contrast, Article 2 allows the offeree to add new terms in the acceptance and in certain situations the new terms can become part of the contract. In order for the new terms to become part of the contract, the following requirements must be met:

a. both parties are merchants.

b. the offer did not provide that additional terms would not be allowed.

c. the new terms do not materially alter the offeror's duties.

d. the offeror does not object within a reasonable time.

Assume the owner of a shrimp farm offers to sell 500 pounds of shrimp to a seafood restaurant chain for two dollars per pound. The restaurant responds: "We accept your offer. Shrimp are to be weighed by certified scales." The shrimp farmer does not object. The new term (requiring weighing by certified scales) becomes part of the contract because it does not materially alter the offeror's duties.

Assume that the restaurant responds: "We accept your offer. Shrimp will be cleaned, deveined and individually packaged in 1 pound plastic wrappings." A contract is formed but the new terms do not become part of the contract because they materially alter the offeror's duties by requiring the cleaning, deveining and packaging of the shrimp.

4. Modification of the contract: Modification or changing the terms of a contract covered by the common law requires new consideration. Assume a contractor agrees to build an office building according to the specifications for an accounting firm for $300,000. During construction, the firm requests the contractor add a patio and the contractor agrees. In order for the firm to enforce the contractor's promise to add the patio, the firm must give new consideration (usually money) to the contractor.

According to Article 2, modification does not require new consideration. Assume an electronic store agrees to sell a cellular phone for $150. The purchaser then requests an additional leather carrying case and the store agrees. The purchaser can enforce the promise for the case even though the purchaser gave no new consideration in exchange for the new promise.

5. Writing Requirement: The **Statute of Frauds** requires that certain contracts must be in writing to be enforceable. Common law contracts that must be in writing include the following: contracts that cannot be performed within one year; marital contracts; contracts to convey interest in real estate; and contracts to answer for the debt of another in case that party defaults.

According to Article 2, contracts for goods priced at $500* or more must be in writing. Exceptions to this writing requirement include the following:

a. When the contract is for specially made goods that cannot be easily resold.

b. When the party being charged admits to entering the contract.

c. When the goods have been accepted or paid for, the contract is enforced to the amount of the accepted goods or the payment accepted.

d. When two merchants enter into a verbal contract and one merchant sends the other a memo confirming the agreement. If the second merchant does not object within ten days, the terms of the memo are enforceable.

Warranties under Article 2: In addition to express warranties created by the seller, the sale of goods may include **Implied Warranties**. These include the implied warranty of fitness for a particular purpose and the implied warranty of merchantability.

* The amended version of UCC 2-201(1) raises the amount to $5,000.

Passage of title and risk of loss under Article 2: Unless the parties provide otherwise, Article 2 applies the following rules regarding the passage of title and risk of loss when goods are transported:

1. Destination contracts: Title and risk of loss do not pass to the buyer until the goods reach the designated destination.

2. Shipment contract: Title and risk of loss pass to the buyer when the goods are delivered to the carrier.

Article 2 and Conditional Sales Contracts: Article 2 recognizes two types of conditional sales:

1. Sale on approval: In this situation, the buyer agrees to purchase the goods after trying them out and approving them. During the time the buyer is trying out the goods (and prior to acceptance) title and risk of loss remain with the seller.

2. Sale or return: In this situation, the buyer purchases the goods for resale; the buyer can return the unsold goods. During the time the goods are in the buyer's place of business, title and risk of loss is on the buyer.

Red Flag Situation

Situation: A bookstore buys 500 copies of a bestseller with the understanding any unsold books can be returned to the publisher A thief breaks into the bookstore and steals all copies of the bestseller.

Potential problem: Risk of loss for the unsold copies was on the bookstore.

Special rules on sale of goods by those who do not own the goods:

1. Sale of goods by a party with void title: Assume a thief breaks into an electronics store and steals a computer. The thief then sells the computer to an insurance agent, who is unaware of the theft. The thief held void title to the computer and therefore had no title to pass on to the insurance agent. The electronics store can reclaim the computer from the agent.

2. Sale of goods by a party with voidable title: A party holds voidable title to goods when the goods were obtained under the following circumstances:

   a. The buyer obtained the goods through fraud.

   b. The buyer obtained the goods with a bad check.

   c. The goods were bought from a minor.

   d. The goods were purchased from an insolvent seller on credit.

A party with voidable title to goods can pass good title to a buyer who is a good faith purchaser and gives value. A good faith purchaser does not know (nor had to reason to know) the seller's title is voidable. The good faith purchaser who buys for value has better rights to the goods than the original seller.

Assume a customer buys a computer from an electronics store and pays with a check that is later dishonored. The customer, who has voidable title, then sells the computer to a neighbor who is unaware of the dishonored check. The electronics store cannot reclaim the computer from the good faith purchaser.

Special entrustment rule: When a customer takes goods in for repair or service to a business that also sells that type of goods, the entrustment rule applies. Assume a customer takes a valuable watch into a shop that both repairs and sells watches. A clerk in the shop inadvertently places the watch in the "sales" cabinet and the watch is sold. The entrustment rule holds that the original owner of the watch cannot reclaim the watch from the buyer who purchases the watch in the ordinary course of business.

Going Global

The United Nations Convention on Contracts for the International Sale of Goods (CISG) applies to the international sale of commercial goods between parties whose places of business are in different countries and those countries have ratified the agreement. The CISG does not apply to consumer goods and does not require a writing. Parties from countries that are signatories to CISG can opt out of its provisions.

Reducing Your Risks

1. If you are a merchant, understand that Article 2 imposes additional responsibilities on the merchant seller. Assume you offer to sell goods to another merchant and the offeree adds additional terms in the acceptance. If you do not object, it is possible that the new terms will become part of the contract.

2. When entering into a sales contract, make certain all of the terms are included in the contract; otherwise, Article 2 can "fill in the blanks" in a manner that may not be satisfactory to you.

3. Carry adequate insurance if you have inventory purchased on a sale or return basis. While the inventory is in your store, risk of loss is on you.

4. When buying goods from another location, make certain you obtain adequate insurance if you are liable for loss while the goods are in transit.

5. Understand the risk of leaving valuable goods with a business that also sells that type of goods; the entrustment rule will apply if your goods are inadvertently sold to a buyer in the ordinary course of business.

6. Make certain you know the origin of goods when purchasing. If the goods are stolen, the true owner can reclaim them from you.

Sources of Information

1. To learn more about Article 2, go to *http://www.swlearning.com/blaw/fundamentals/fundamentals6e/fundamentals6e.html*. Go to "Interactive Study Guide" and click on Chapter 15, "Title and Loss."

2. Information on international sales of goods is available from Pace University's Institute of International Commercial Law at *http://www.cisg.law.pace.edu*.

Security Agreement

(For additional information, *see Financing Statement* and *Secured Transactions.*)

A *security agreement* is a document signed by a debtor granting the creditor security rights in specified collateral.

Requirements for a security agreement: Section 9 of the Uniform Commercial Code (UCC) regulates security agreements. The agreement must: (1) be in a writing or authentication signed by the debtor; (2) describe the collateral; and (3) reasonably identify the specific collateral. (UCC 9-203, 9-110).

Subject matter of collateral: The collateral identified in the security agreement may include property the debtor currently possesses, after-acquired property, proceeds from the sale of the collateral, and future advances provided by a continuing line of credit.

Red Flag Situation

Situation: A lending institution loans $1million to a car dealership for the purchase of new autos. The security agreement lists only the autos as collateral. The dealership sells all of its inventory and then defaults on the loan.

Potential problem: The security agreement did not include proceeds from the sale of the inventory as collateral. The creditor therefore has no collateral right to the proceeds.

Going Global

Laws regarding secured transactions vary widely throughout the world. If your company sells goods on credit or lends money abroad, become familiar with the host country's laws on secured transactions.

Reducing Your Risks

1. If your company is in the business of selling on credit or lending money, make certain the security agreement signed by the debtor complies with UCC requirements.

2. Confirm that the collateral listed in the security agreement adequately protects your company's interest in case the debtor defaults.

Sources of Information

1. Cornell offers information on secured transactions at *http://www.law.cornell. edu/topics/secured_transactions.html.*

2. For more information on secured transactions, go to *http://www.swlearning. com/blaw/fundamentals/fundamentals6e/fundamentals6e.html.* Go to "Interactive Study Center" and click on Chapter 20, "Secured Transactions."

Secured Transaction

(For additional information, *see Financing Statement* and *Security Agreement.*)

In a *secured transaction*, the creditor has the right to foreclose on certain assets of the debtor in case of default. Article 9 of the Uniform Commercial Code (UCC) applies to secured transactions.

Steps involved in a secured transaction are attachment and perfection.

1. Attachment refers to the creation of the security interest. Attachment occurs in the following ways:

    a. The creditor retains possession of the collateral until the debt is paid.

    b. The debtor signs a security agreement granting the creditor interest in specified collateral.

2. Perfection occurs when the creditor gives notice of interest in the collateral, thereby protecting the creditor's interest against claims by others. Perfection may occur in three ways:

    a. The creditor retains possession of the collateral until the debt is paid.

    b. The debtor signs a financing statement, which is filed in the proper governmental office.

    c. Perfection occurs automatically when the loan involves a purchase money security interest (PMSI) in consumer goods (except for boats, vehicles and trailers, which must meet state requirements regarding title). Even when perfection is automatic, the creditor may lose rights in the collateral unless a financing statement is filed.

A PMSI arises in two situations: (1) the creditor sells the collateral to the debtor on credit or (2) the creditor loans money to the debtor for the purchase of a specific asset.

Continuations Statements: According to the UCC, the original financing statement is valid for sixty months and must be renewed in order to continue.

Red Flag Situation

Situation: A bank loans an accounting firm $200,000 to purchase a new computer system. The loan is to be repaid over 72 months. The bank files a financing statement in the proper office when the loan is created but fails to file a continuation statement before the sixty months expire. Sixty-two months after obtaining the loan the firm defaults. The bank attempts to foreclose on the computer system.

Potential problem: The original financing statement was valid for five years. By failing to file a continuation statement, the bank loses its right in the collateral after five years.

Taking Possession of the Collateral: The UCC provides that unless the parties agreed otherwise, the creditor can take possession of the collateral upon default unless the action will be a "breach of the peace." (UCC 9-503) The UCC does not explain "breach of the peace." Prior to repossessing collateral, the creditor should seek advice on what is considered peaceful action within the jurisdiction.

Red Flag Situation

Situation: An electronics store sells a $500 television to a consumer on credit. The customer defaults after paying $400 of the debt. The store repossess the set and retains it.

Potential problem: When the debtor has paid at least 60 percent of the debt for a consumer good, the creditor cannot retain the collateral after repossession. The creditor must give proper notice to the debtor and other secured parties and then sell the collateral in a reasonable manner. Any money received in excess of the amount due and expenses is returned to the debtor.

Going Global

1. Laws regarding secured transactions vary greatly throughout the world.

2. In order to reduce the risk of nonpayment for goods, many international sellers insist on a documentary sale where the buyer pays the collecting bank when the buyer is presented with certain negotiable documents.

Reducing Your Risks

1. When your company extends credit or lends money, make certain the security agreement is prepared in accordance with the UCC. File the financing statement immediately with the proper governmental office.

2. If the debt extends more than 60 months, make certain a continuation statement is filed.

3. If collateral must be repossessed, confirm that the repossession process will be in a peaceful manner.

4. When selling goods on credit abroad, consider the benefits of a documentary sale.

Sources of Information

1. Information on creditor rights is available at *http://www.law.cornell.edu/topics/debtor_creditor.html*.

2. Secured transactions are discussed at *http://www.swlearning.com/blaw/fundamentals/fundamentals6e/fundamentals6e.html*. Go to "Internet Applications" and click on Chapter 20, "Secured Transactions."

Sexual Harrassment

(For additional information, *see Civil Rights Act of 1964*.)

According to Title VII of the Civil Rights Act of 1964, *sexual harassment* occurs in the workplace in two ways: (1) the injured party is placed in a "quid pro quo" situation or (2) the injured party is subjected to a hostile work environment. Title VII applies to harassment by members of the same sex and by members of the opposite sex. Employers are also subject to state anti-discrimination laws.

Quid Pro Quo Harassment: The Latin phrase "quid pro quo" refers to the exchange of one favor for another. This type of sexual harassment occurs when the complainant is offered advantages in the workplace in exchange for sexual favors. As a general rule, the courts have held that the employer is liable for quid pro quo harassment by a supervisor or another employee even though the employer did not know (and had no reason to know) of the harassment.

Hostile Work Environment: According to the courts, a hostile work environment exists when an employee is subjected to discriminatory intimidation and ridicule to such an extent that the workplace conditions become abusive. The existence of a hostile work environment is addressed on a case-by-case basis. The court may hold the employer liable even if the employer did not know of the situation. The employer may also be liable if it has no policy against sexual harassment or has failed to inform employees of an existing policy.

Sexual Harassment by a Party not Associated with the Employer: An employer may be liable when an employee is subjected to sexual harassment by a non-employee (customer, client, etc.) if the employer knew or should have known of the harassment and took no action to stop it.

Red Flag Situation

Situation: A female accountant with a firm is regularly subjected to discriminatory remarks by a client. She complains to her employer. The employer does not want to offend one of its best clients and takes no action.

Potential problem: Once the employer knew (or should have known) of the female accountant's hostile work environment, the employer had a duty to stop the harassment. By failing to take action, the employer can be held liable.

Going Global

1. Title VII of the Civil Rights Act of 1964 applies abroad when the complainant is an American citizen and the company is under the control of an American employer.

2. Many countries have laws addressing sexual harassment in the workplace today.

Reducing Your Risks

1. Be familiar with the current Equal Employment Opportunity Commission (EEOC) guidelines relative to sexual harassment as well as your state's employment discrimination regulations.

2. Make certain your company has an established policy regarding sexual harassment and a complaint procedure and these are distributed to all employees.

3. Caution supervisors to act immediately on any employee's complaints of being subjected to sexual harassment by other employees or outsiders.

4. Make certain your company complies with all federal and state regulations regarding the required posting of certain information relative to discrimination in the workplace.

5. If your company is in control of operations abroad, understand that Title VII applies to U.S. citizens working in the operation.

Sources of Information

1. To learn more about Title VII, visit the federal Equal Employment Opportunity Commission at *http://www.eeoc.gov*.

2. The federal Department of Labor addresses sexual harassment at *http://www.dol.gov*.

3. Information regarding you state's employment discrimination laws are available through the web cite of the state's Office of Attorney General.

4. More information is available at *http://www.swlearning.com/blaw/ fundamentals/fundamentals6e/fundamentals6e.html*. Go to "Court Case Updates" and click on "Employment Law." Also go to "Internet Applications" and click on Chapter 24, "Employment Law."

Slander

(For additional information, *see **Defamation** and **Torts**.*)

The intentional tort of ***slander*** is a category of ***defamation*** that involves a verbal (spoken) statement that injures the plaintiff's reputation.

Requirements for slander: In order for the plaintiff to prevail in a slander suit, the plaintiff must prove the following:

1. The defendant made a false statement.

2. The statement is harmful to plaintiff's reputation.

3. The statement was published (spoken) to at least one other person. If a third party overhears the defendant making the false statement to the plaintiff, the publication requirement is met.

Defenses

1. Truth is the ultimate defense in a defamation suit.

2. Privilege refers to certain statements that, although defamatory, are protected. Protected statements include those made by attorneys in courtroom proceedings and statements made by members of the U. S. Congress during debate on the floors of Congress.

3. In addition, absence of malice is a defense when the plaintiff is a public figure. In this situation, the plaintiff must prove malice on the defendant's part. Malice means that the defendant either (a) knew the statement was false or (b) made the state-

ment with reckless disregard for the truth.

Red Flag Situations

1. *Situation:* The office manager of a financial firm verbally accuses an employee of overstating her expenditures on a travel voucher. The manager's secretary overhears the accusation. The employee later proves the voucher was accurate. *Potential problem:* The firm may be liable for the manager's slander because the tort was committed within the scope of employment. (For more information on employer's liability, see *Agency*.)

2. *Situation:* A retail clerk suspects a customer has just shoplifted a hand-held computer. The clerk yells, "Stop, thief!" Several shoppers hear the clerk. The accused did not shoplift any item. *Potential problem:* The customer may sue for slander based on the clerk's accusation. The employer faces liability because the tort occurred "within the scope of employment."

Going Global

1. Defamation laws (including the laws on slander) vary throughout the world.

2. Many countries recognize the employer's liability for the torts of an employee committed with the scope of employment.

Reducing Your Risks

1. Make certain employees are not verbally accused of wrongdoing unless the accusation can be confirmed. If the accusation was heard by a third party and is later proven to be false, the victim can sue for slander.

2. Advise employees who deal with third parties (customers, clients, etc.) of the potential liability of falsely accusing the party of wrongdoing.

Sources of Information

1. To learn more, go to *http://www.swlearning.com/blaw/fundamentals/fundamentals6e/fundamentals6e.html.* Go to "Interactive Study Center" and click on Chapter 4, "Torts and Cybertorts."

2. Additional information on slander and other torts is available at *http://www.law.cornell.edu/topics/torts.html.*

Statue of Frauds

(For additional information, *see* **Contract** and **Sales**.)

The **statute of frauds** requires that certain contracts must be in writing to be enforceable. Each state has its own statute of frauds. In addition, Article 2 of the Uniform Commercial Code (UCC) requires that certain contracts for the sale of goods must be in writing.

Contracts that Must be in Writing: The Statute of Frauds generally covers the following contracts:

1. contracts that cannot possibly be performed within one year. The one-year period begins to run the day following the formation of the contract;

2. contracts involving real property, including mortgages, sales, and leases of land;

3. marital contracts;

4. collateral contracts where a party guarantees to pay the debt of another if the original debtor defaults; and

5. contracts to sell goods priced at $500 or more. (UCC 2-201) (According to the amended version of UCC 2-201, the amount is $5,000.)

Red Flag Situation

Situation: A customer applies for a loan from a lending institution. Due to the customer's poor credit rating, the lender requires a guarantor to promise to pay the loan in case the debtor defaults. A wealthy relative verbally guarantees the loan. The debtor defaults and the lender requests payment from the relative, who refuses to pay.

Potential problem: A guaranty contract (where a party promises to be secondarily liable on another's debt) is covered by the Statute of Frauds. The lending institution cannot enforce the verbal promise.

Exceptions to the Writing Requirement: A court will enforce a verbal contract covered by the Statute of Frauds in the following situations:

1. If a party has partially performed. Assume a retailer verbally agrees to purchase $700 in goods. The manufacturer delivers $400 in goods immediately and the retailer accepts. The retailer has partially performed by accepting the order and must pay $400.

2. Some jurisdictions hold that if a party admits in judicial proceedings to the existence of a contract, the contract is enforceable against that party.

3. Promissory estoppel. The doctrine of promissory estoppel holds that if a party makes a promise knowing the other party will rely on it and the other party does justifiably rely on the promise, the relying party can enforce the promise (even though the victim did not give consideration). Some jurisdictions hold that a verbal promise covered by the Statute of Frauds is still enforceable if promissory estoppel applies.

4. UCC exceptions to the writing requirement. According to Article 2, verbal contracts for goods priced at $500 or more (or $5,000 or more according to the amended UCC) are still enforceable in the following circumstances: (a) the goods are specially manufactured and cannot be easily resold; (b) the parties have partially performed; and (c) a party admits to the contract.

The Form of Writing Required: The Statute of Frauds does not require any particular form of writing. Generally an invoice, fax, memo or sales slip is sufficient if it names the parties and the subject matter, states the essential terms and is signed by the person to be charged. State laws regarding transfer of real property may require a deed contain additional information.

Special Rules for the Sale of Goods Contracts: According to Article 2, a verbal contract for goods priced at $500 ($5,000 according to the amended UCC) or more is enforceable if (1) both parties are merchants'; (2) one party sends a memo confirming the verbal agreement; and (3) the other party does not object within ten days.

Going Global

1. Most countries require certain contract must be in writing to be enforceable.

2. The United Nations Convention on the International Sale of Goods (CISG) does not require a writing for any contract covered by the convention.

Reducing Your Risks

1. The safest approach is to require a written contract even if the Statute of Frauds does not cover the agreement. This can avoid later disputes as to what each party said.

2. Review your state's Statute of Frauds to assure compliance.

3. Prior to signing any contract, read it carefully. If you do not understand any provisions, seek competent counsel.

4. If your company uses standard "boiler-plate" contracts when dealing with employees, clients, etc., make certain the written contract is legally enforceable.

5. Never enter into a written contract when the other party is trying to rush you into the agreement. In an equitable situation, the other party will want to make certain

you understand all terms of the contract.

Sources of Information

1. To learn more, go to *http://www.swlearning.com/blaw/fundamentals/fundamentals6e/fundamentals6e.html*. Go to "Interactive Study Center" and click on Chapter 10, "Defenses Agains Contract Enforceability."

2. To access the UCC for your state, go to *http://www.lac.cornell.edu*. Then select your state and click on "Commercial Code."

Strict Liability

(For additional information, *see Agency, Product Liability*, and *Torts*.)

The area of tort law called *strict liability* is also referred to as "liability without fault." In certain circumstances, a court will find a defendant liable even though there was no wrongful intent or negligence on the defendant's part.

When *strict liability* applies: According to tort law, strict liability applies in two situations:

1. When the defendant engages in an ultra hazardous activity; or

2. When the injured party claims product liability. Imposition of strict liability is a policy decision based on the potential for extensive physical injuries and property damage.

Ultra Hazardous Activity: The courts may apply strict liability when the defendant engages in an extremely dangerous or exceptional activity that has the potential to cause great harm to others. Examples of these activities include blasting operations, fumigation, transporting hazardous materials and keeping dangerous animals.

Red Flag Situation

Situation: A fumigation company contracts to fumigate a three-story office building. The building shares a "common wall" with the adjacent building. Unknown to the fumigator, there is a hole in the common wall. All workers in the first building are evacuated for 24 hours. Due to the hole, the toxic fumes escape into the second building, causing serious injury to its occupants.

Potential problem: The fumigation company can be held strictly liable although there was no wrongdoing (intent or negligence) on its part.

Product liability: In order to prevail in a strict product liability claim, the plaintiff must prove the following:

1. The product was defective when it left the defendant.

2. The product was not substantially changed from the time of sale until the injury.

3. The defect was the proximate (foreseeable) cause of physical or property damage to the plaintiff.

4. Most states also require that the defect rendered the product unreasonably dangerous. Defects may occur in the manufacture, design, or provision of warnings regarding the product.

Red Flag Situation

Situation: A domestic chain of toy stores sells dolls imported from abroad. Unknown to the retailer, the dolls' faces are painted with a toxic substance. A number of children become ill from the substance. Their parents sue the retailer based on strict product liability.

Potential problem: All parties in the distribution chain, including the retailer, face potential liability in a product liability case.

Defenses Available in Product Liability Cases: Defenses available include:

1. assumption of risk;

2. misuse of the product;

3. comparative or contributory negligence; and

4. the injury was due to a "commonly known danger." Courts have held there is a duty to warn of the dangers of misuse if the manufacturer knew or should have known of the potential misuse.

Going Global

Many countries recognize the doctrine of strict liability today. The elements the plaintiff must prove vary in different countries.

Reducing Your Risks

1. Understand that if your company is in the business of selling or leasing products, you face potential product liability even if the product arrived at your business sealed and was never altered.

2. Make certain the manufacturer of the goods you lease or sell is a responsible party. If you are sued for product liability, you will need to seek indemnification.

3. If your company engages in ultra hazardous activities, confirm that the company is

carrying adequate liability insurance.

Sources of Information

1. Information on product liability is available from the American Law Institute at *http://www.ali.org.*

2. For more information on strict liability, go to *http://www.swlearning.com/blaw/ fundamentals/fundamentals6e/fundamentals6e.html.* Go to "Internet Applications" and click on Chapter 17, "Warranties and Product Liability."

Tt

Title Insurance

(For additional information, *see* **Insurance**.)

Title insurance represents a contract where the insurer (the title company) promises to defend any subsequent claims to real property (land) that are not noted as exceptions in the title policy issued by the insurer. Lending institutions generally require a title policy before issuing a loan for the purchase of real property in order to assure the seller has marketable title to the property. Zoning restrictions and easements do not make the title unmarketable. Prior to issuing the policy, the insurer searches the legal records in the county where the property is located for any encumbrances to title (liens, mortgages, etc.).

Red Flag Situation

Situation: A retail store decides to purchase the adjacent land for cash. The seller assures the buyer there is no need for a title insurance policy. (The seller ordinarily pays for the policy). Following the purchase, a relative of the seller claims to be the true owner and sues the retail store.

Potential problem: The defendant must incur the cost of defending the lawsuit. If the plaintiff prevails, the defendant may lose title to the property.

Going Global

1. Insurance laws vary greatly throughout the world. Title insurance is not available in all countries.

2. Even if a party obtains a title policy, the risk of confiscation by the host country may still exist. Many companies investing abroad obtain political risk insurance for this reason.

Reducing Your Risks

1. Always insist on a title policy when buying real property.

2. When investing in property abroad, consider also obtaining political risk insurance if possible.

3. Make certain you understand any exceptions listed on the title policy; they may impact your plans for the future use of the property.

Sources of Information

1. To learn more about title insurance, go to *http://www.swlearning.com/blaw/fundamentals/fundamentals6e/fundamentals6e.html*. Go to "Interactive Study Center" and click on Chapter 31, "Insurance, Wills, and Trusts."

2. Information about political risk insurance is available from *http://www.opic.gov*.

Tort

(For additional information, see *Assault, Battery, Defamation, Disparagement of Property, False Imprisonment, Fraud, Intentional Infliction of Emotional Distress, Libel, Negligence, Product Liability, Slander, Strict Liability, Trade Libel, Trespass, Wrongful Interference with a Contractual Relationship* and *Wrongful Interference with an Economic Expectation*.)

A *tort* is a private wrong committed against the injured party's person or property. The word "tort" comes from the French term meaning "twisted." Tort cases are brought in civil court (rather than criminal court) and a private attorney represents the plaintiff.

Categories of torts: Tort law is divided into three categories: intentional torts, negligence and strict liability.

1. *Intentional torts:* When the defendant actually intends the action that results in harm to the plaintiff, the tort is classified as intentional even though the defendant did not intend to harm the victim. The following intentional torts impact today's

business environment:

a. **Assault:** This intentional tort is different from the crime of assault. The tort of assault requires four elements: (i) the defendant intentionally commits the act which threatens or places the plaintiff in fear; (ii) the harm perceived or feared is imminent; (iii) the plaintiff experiences apprehension; and (iv) the apprehension is reasonable. For a complete discussion of this intentional tort, *see* the topic *Assault*.

b. **Battery:** The tort of battery requires the following elements: (i) the defendant or an extension of defendant intentionally touches plaintiff; (ii) the touching is without plaintiff's consent; (iii) the touching is offensive to plaintiff; and (iv) the touching would be offensive to a person of normal sensibilities. For a complete discussion, *see* the topic *Battery*.

Defenses to Assault and Battery: Defenses to these torts include consent and defense of oneself or others (if real or apparent danger is present).

c. **Defamation:** Defamation refers to a false statement that is harmful to plaintiff's personal or business reputation and is published to at least one other person. The two categories of defamation are libel (the written statement) and slander (the spoken statement). For a complete discussion, *see* the topics *Defamation, Disparagement of Property, Libel and Slander*.

Defenses to Defamation: Defenses include truth, privilege, and absence of malice (when the plaintiff is a public figure).

d. **Invasion of Privacy:** This intentional tort can occur in the following ways:

i. Disclosing private information about the plaintiff that would be objectionable to an ordinary purpose. Assume a local newspaper runs a story disclosing that a private citizen was expelled from college for cheating twenty years earlier. Although the story is true, a court may find there is no overwhelming need for the public to know this information and the paper is liable for invasion of privacy.

ii. Appropriation: Using an individual's name, voice-alike or image to indorse a product or service for gain without permission can result in a lawsuit claiming appropriation.

Red Flag Situation

Situation: A computer software company runs an advertisement on television using a model that strikingly resembles a sports celebrity. The ad shows the model using the software program on a home computer. The celebrity sues for appropriation. The defendant responds it never used the celebrity's name in the ad. *Potential problem:* If the public is likely to believe the model is in fact the plaintiff, the tort of appropriation has occurred. Courts have also held that using a "sound-alike" with a voice closely resembling a celebrity's can also result in appropriation.

    iii. Intrusion into one's private affairs or invading one's seclusion: A supervisor eavesdropping on an employee's private telephone conversation violates this right of privacy.

    iv. Publishing information that places the plaintiff in a false light: If a newspaper runs an article indicating an executive endorses a political candidate when the executive does not, the executive may sue for being placed in a false light.

e. *False imprisonment:* This tort involves the deprivation of one's freedom of movement. Businesses that detain suspected shoplifters are sometimes sued if the accused proves no items were taken.

Merchant's defense: All states have passed statutes granting protection (privilege) for merchants who detain suspected shoplifters if certain requirements are met. Generally theses statutes provide the merchant is not liable for detaining a suspected shoplifter who did not in fact take items if the following requirements are met: (i) the defendant had reasonable grounds to suspect shoplifting; (ii) the suspect was detained in a reasonable manner; and (iii) the detention was for a reasonable period of time. For a complete discussion, *see* the topic *False Imprisonment*.

f. *Fraud:* The following elements are required for plaintiff to prevail:

    i. the defendant made a false or misleading statement of fact;

    ii. the defendant knew the statement was false or made it with reckless disregard for the truth;

    iii. the statement was material to the plaintiff;

    iv. the plaintiff justifiably relied on the statement; and

    v. the plaintiff suffered damages due to the reliance.

For a complete discussion, *see* the topic *Fraud*.

f. *Intentional infliction of emotional distress:* This tort occurs when the defendant engages in an outrageous activity intended to cause the plaintiff to suffer a high degree of emotional distress. For a complete discussion, see the topic *Intentional Infliction of Emotional Distress*.)

g. *Wrong interference with a contractual relationship:* To prevail, the plaintiff must prove the following three elements:

    i. the plaintiff had an existing contractual relationship with a third party;

    ii. the defendant knew of this relationship; and

    iii. the defendant knowingly interfered with the contract for the defendant's own monetary gain.

Red Flag Situation

Situation: The human resource director of an architectural firm is looking for new architects to boost the firm's sagging income. Aware that the top architect in the city has a five-year contract with a competitor, the director approaches the architect and talks her into leaving her current employer and joining the firm.

Potential problem: The former employer may successfully sue the firm for wrongful interference with a contractual relationship. (The plaintiff may also sue the architect for breach of contract.)

    i. ***Wrongful interference with an economic expectation:*** This tort is based on interfering with a relationship the plaintiff has with a potential customer or client that may result in an economic benefit.

Red Flag Situation

Situation: A customer is looking at new cars at a local dealership. A representative of a competing company enters, approaches the customer, and persuades the customer to leave the dealership and shop with the competition.

Potential problem: The competing company may be liable for wrongful interference with an economic benefit based on its representative's predatory action.

    j. ***Wrongfully entering business:*** This tort occurs when a party establishes a new business with no legitimate business purpose and with the sole intent to harm another party's business. The court will hold the defendant liable for the predatory action.

    k. ***Trespass:*** Intentionally interfering with a party's right to enjoy her property can result in liability for trespass. The interference may involve real property or personal (moveable) property.

Trespass to real property: The owner or possessor of real estate must usually establish the defendant as a trespasser. This may be accomplished by posting a sign such as "No Trespassing" on the property. When the defendant enters the property for an illegal purpose, however, the culprit is considered a trespasser regardless of whether a sign was posted. The plaintiff does not have to prove harm to the property.

Red Flag Situation

Situation: A real estate company has been the frequent target of attempted night-time burglaries. The company owner places dangerous dogs on the premises. While attempting to break in one night, a trespasser is severely injured by the dogs.

Potential problem: Many courts now hold that the possessor or owner of property must post a notice regarding guard dogs; otherwise, the property owner may be liable to the trespasser for injuries caused by the dogs. (Courts have also held property owners liable for "booby traps" which cause injuries to trespassers.)

Trespass to personal property: Interfering with one's enjoyment or possession of personal property is also referred to as "trespass for personalty."

1. *Infringement on intellectual property rights:* Infringing on another's intellectual property rights (patents, copyrights, trademarks and trade secrets) is considered an intentional tort.

2. *Negligence:* The four elements required for the unintentional tort of negligence are the following:

   a. the defendant owed a duty to the plaintiff;

   b. the defendant breached (broke) that duty;

   c. the breach was the actual and proximate (foreseeable) cause; and

   d. of the injuries the plaintiff suffered.

(For a complete discuss of negligence, *see* the topic *Negligence*.)

3. *Strict Liability:* This area of tort liability is also referred to as liability without fault. Strict liability is imposed in two situations:

   a. When the defendant undertakes an ultra hazardous activity such as fumigation, crop dusting, transporting hazardous cargo, or keeping a dangerous animal

   b. When certain defective goods are sold. In the area of strict product liability, all parties in the distribution change face potential liability.

(For a complete discussion, *see Strict Liability*.)

Going Global

1. Tort law varies greatly throughout the world. Many countries today recognize strict liability for certain types of activities.

2. In many civil law countries, tort liability is found under the codal articles discussing "Obligations."

3. Many countries recognize the concept of "respondeat superior" holding that the

employer is liable for the torts committed by an employee "within the scope of employment."

Reducing Your Risks

1. Understand that the employer can be liable for a tort committed by an employee "within the scope of employment."

2. If your company is engaged in ultra hazardous activities that can lead to strict liability, make certain you carry adequate liability insurance.

3. If you are in the business of selling or leasing goods, remember that all merchants in the distribution chain face potential liability if a consumer brings a product liability case. It is therefore important to deal with manufacturers who are responsible and will still be in business in the event a lawsuit is filed.

Sources of Information

1. Information on tort liability is available at *http://www.swlearning.com/blaw/fundamentals/fundamentals6e/fundamentals6e.html*. Go to "Interactive Study Center" and click on Chapter 4, "Tort and Cyber Torts."

2. To learn more about product liability, visit the American Law Institute at *http://www.ali.org*.

Trade Libel

(For additional information, *see Defamation, Disparagement of Property*, and *Torts*.)

The intentional tort involving defamatory statements regarding the quality of another party's products is referred to as slander of quality or trade libel. This tort comes under the category of *disparagement of property* and is discussed under that topic.

Trade Secret

(For more information, *see Copyrights, Covenant Not to Compete, Intellectual Property, Patents, Property* and *Trademarks*.)

A *trade secret* is a form of intellectual property consisting of any information that a business entity has that provides it with an advantage over the competition. Examples include marketing plans, customer lists, formulas, recipes, and expansion plans. Businesses sometimes choose to treat certain intellectual property (such as a formula) as a trade secret rather than obtaining a patent due to the worldwide availability of patent information today via the Internet.

Criminal Sanctions for Theft of Trade Secrets: The federal Economic Espionage Act of 1996 (the Act) (18 U.S.C. §§ 1831-1839) criminalizes the theft of trade secrets. In addition, purchasing or possessing another party's trade secrets when aware they were acquired without the legal owner's permission is also a federal crime. Individuals guilty under the Act face up to ten years in prison and $500,000 in fines. Corporations face up to $5 million in fines. Any property used to acquire the trade secret (i.e., computers) can be confiscated by the government.

Civil Sanctions: The Uniform Trade Secrets Act allows a plaintiff to recover up to double the amount of damages suffered plus court costs and attorney fees if the defendant willfully and maliciously misappropriated the secrets. Over forty states have now adopted some form of the uniform act. A plaintiff also has the option of bringing a civil suit alleging trade secret infringement.

Protection of Trade Secrets: Businesses today frequently request employees with access to trade secrets to sign two agreements:

1. In a "nondisclosure agreement" the employee agrees to refrain from divulging any company trade secrets.

2. A covenant not to compete agreement provides that if the employee leaves the present employer, the worker will not compete in a specified geographic area for a specific time span.

Red Flag Situation

Situation: A stockbroker leaves a major financial firm and joins a competitor. The broker, who signed a nondisclosure agreement with the first employer, takes a customer list to the new employer. The latter immediately uses the list. ***Potential problem:*** Both the broker and the new employer may face criminal liability under the Economic Espionage Act and civil liability under the Uniform Trade Secrets Act if the state has adopted the latter Act.

Going Global

1. In a majority of countries, theft of trade secrets is a serious crime.

2. The North American Free Trade Agreement (NAFTA) requires all members (Canada, Mexico, and the United States) to take measures to protect trade secrets.

3. The Economic Espionage Act of 1996 applies to conduct outside the U.S. if;

    a. the offender is a natural person who is a citizen or permanent resident alien of the United States, or an organization organized under the laws of the United States or a State or political subdivision thereof; or

2. an act in furtherance of the offense was committed in the United States. (18 U.S.C. § 1837)

Reducing Your Risks

1. Seek advice from an intellectual property attorney to confirm your company is taking the necessary steps to establish certain information as trade secrets.

2. Review the physical measures your company is taking to protect trade secrets (i.e., safes, security systems, inventory procedures).

3. Make certain that any information your company obtains does not infringe on another party's trade secrets.

4. Recognize the need for vigilance in monitoring your company's trade secrets both domestically and internationally.

Sources of Information

1. To learn more about trade secrets, visit *http://www.law.cornell.edu*. Go to "Law by Source or Jurisdiction–Federal Law." Then enter "18 U.S.C. 1831."

2. Additional information is available at *http://www.swlearning.com/blaw/fundamentals/fundamentals6e/fundamentals6e.html*. Go to "Interactive Study Center" and click on Chapter 5, "Intellectual Property and Internet Law."

Trademark

A *trademark* is a form of intellectual property consisting of a distinctive name, word, device, or symbol that identifies a specific product. Businesses offering services are identified by service marks. Both trademarks and service marks are protected in the same manner.

Applicable Statutory Law: The Lanham Trademark Act of 1946 (15 U.S.C. §§ 1051-1128) provides for federal trademark and service mark protection. The Lanham Act was amended in 1995 by the Federal Trademark Dilution Act. The latter act provides that a plaintiff no longer has to show either that the unauthorized use of a protected mark is by a business in competition with the plaintiff or that the use is likely to confuse the public.

Red Flag Situation

Situation: A sports shoe company's registered trademark includes the slogan "Over the Top." A banking institution begins using the same slogan in its television advertisements.

Potential problem: The sports shoe company may sue for trademark dilution. According to the Federal Trademark Dilution Act, the injured party does not have to show the defendant is in the same type of business as the plaintiff and does not have to show that the public is likely to be confused and believe the shoe company is affiliated with the bank. The court may hold that the defendant's use of the slogan "dilutes" the uniqueness of the slogan. (In addition to the federal dilution law, a majority of the states have now passed similar laws.)

Obtaining Trademark Protection: Owners of trademarks may register their marks with the federal government or the state. For federal protection, the applicant registers with the U.S. Patent and Trademark Office. Federal trademark protection is valid for 20 years and is renewable.

Subject Matter for Trademark Protection: In order to receive trademark protection under the Lanham Act, the applicant must show the trademark is distinctive enough so customers can easily identify it. As a general rule, personal names and geographic or descriptive terms do not receive trademark protection unless they have obtained a secondary meaning. The personal names "Ralph Lauren" and "Liz Claiborne" are examples of personal names that have attained secondary meanings (identifiable with specific items) and therefore received trademark protection.

Trademark Protection for Product Colors: In 1995, the U.S. Supreme Court ruled that in certain circumstances a business can obtain trademark protection for a color that is specifically identified with its product. The Court ruled that a color could be identified as a product's "symbol" and identify the product to the public. The Court pointed out that trademark protection had already been afforded for the shape of product's containers and unique sounds associated with a company.

Trade Dress: The overall appearance of a business or product is referred to as trade dress. In 1992, the U.S. Supreme Court heard a case involving the alleged infringement of the trade dress (architectural design, décor, menu, etc.) of a restaurant. The Court ruled for the plaintiff, finding that trade dress infringement is also protected.

Red Flag Situation

Situation: A national banking chain is easily identifiable by the unique design of its buildings, the bronze front doors and the red striped awnings from the doors to the sidewalks. A competing financial institution builds a structure strikingly similar.

Potential problem: The chain may sue for trade dress infringement, alleging the defendant's bank is so similar in appearance that the public may become confused as to ownership.

Going Global

1. The Paris Convention for the Protection of Industrial Property requires that signatory nations provide the same trademark protection to citizens of other signatory nations that it affords its own citizens.

2. The European Union (EU) established a Community Trademark System in 1996 providing that a trademark application filed in one EU country is protected in all EU countries.

3. According to the General Agreement of Tariffs and Trade (GTT), a trademark will not be issued for alcoholic beverages if the trademark has misleading information regarding geographic origin.

4. The International Trademark Association (INTA) provides assistance to businesses from over 120 countries regarding international protection of trademarks.

5. Trademark laws are not vigorously enforced in some parts of the world.

Reducing Your Risks

1. Make certain any of your company's identifiable marks are properly registered for trademark protection.

2. Commerce must be put into use within a specified period of time. Be careful that you do not lose trademark protection through nonuse.

3. Consult with an intellectual property attorney to make certain your trademarks are protected both domestically and internationally.

4. Recognize the need to monitor for trademark infringements both at home and abroad.

5. When selecting a name or logo for a new product, be careful that you are not infringing or diluting another party's trademark.

6. When choosing the design, décor, signage, etc. for your new business, avoid trade dress infringement.

7. Remember to renew your trademarks.

8. Monitor the use of names and slogans currently protected by trademarks to make certain they do not become generic terms and lose their protection. Once a word is used generically, it is no longer eligible for trademark protection. Words that

were once protected but are now considered generic include nylon, corn flakes, linoleum and aspirin.

Sources of Information

1. To learn more about trademarks, visit the Cyberspace Law Institute at *http://www.cli.org.*

2. Cornell School of Law provides trademark information at *http://www.law.cornell.edu/topics/trademarks.html.*

3. The U. S. Patent and Trademark Office includes a Question and Answer section and links to statutes at *http://www.uspto.gov.*

4. Information on international trademarks protection can be found at http://wipo.int and *http://www.wto.org.*

5. More is available at *http://www.swlearning.com/blaw/fundamentals/fundamentals6e/fundamentals6e.html.* Go to "Interactive Study Center" and click on Chapter 5. "Intellectual Property and Internet Law."

Trespass

The intentional tort of trespass involves the interference with one's right to use or enjoy real or personal property. For a complete discussion, *see* "Intentional Torts" under the topic *Torts*.

Uu

Unemployment Insurance

(For additional information, *see **Insurance**.*)

Unemployment insurance is available for a specified period of time to qualified workers who lose their jobs. Workers who voluntarily quit or are dismissed for wrongful behavior are not eligible.

Applicable Statutes: The Federal Unemployment Tax Act of 1935 (26 U.S.C. §§ 3301-3310) established the federal unemployment insurance system that is administered by the individual states. Employers covered by the Act pay unemployment taxes regularly.

Going Global

1. Employment laws vary greatly throughout the world. Many countries require employers contribute to a government-administered unemployment insurance program.

2. Tenured workers in some countries are entitled to unemployment pay based on the number of years they have worked for a company.

Reducing Your Risks

1. Understand that you must comply with both federal and state law regarding unem-

ployment insurance for your workers.

2. If you hire employees abroad, be certain that you understand the host country's laws regarding unemployment insurance. Noncompliance carries heavy sanctions in some countries.

Sources of Information

1. To learn more about unemployment insurance, go to *http://www.swlearning.com /blaw/fundamentals/fundamentals6e/fundamentals6e.html*. Go to "Interactive Study Center" and click on Chapter 23, "Employment Law."

2. The American Federation of Labor-Congress of Industrial Organizations discusses unemployment benefits at *http://www.aflcio.org*.

Vv

Vehicle Insurance

(For additional information, *see **Insurance**.*)

Businesses ordinarily purchase **vehicle insurance** to cover losses due to property damage and bodily injury resulting from the use of business autos, vans and trucks.

Specific Areas of Coverage: Vehicle insurance policies ordinarily include the following areas of coverage:

1. **Liability coverage:** Liability arising from bodily injury and property damage resulting from an accident is included.

2. **Collision and comprehensive coverage:** The insured's vehicle is covered in case of a collision. Damage resulting from causes other than collisions (hail, theft, wind, etc.) is included in the comprehensive coverage.

3. **No-fault insurance:** In states that allow no-fault coverage, the policyholder files a claim against his own insurer no matter which party caused the accident.

4. **Uninsured motorist coverage:** This provision covers a driver and passengers when injured by an uninsured motorist or in a hit-and-run incident.

5. **Medical payment coverage**: Medical bills are covered for all those in the insured's vehicle.

6. *Accidental death coverage:* If the insured is killed, a lump sum is provided to beneficiaries.

7. *Other-driver coverage:* The vehicle owner is protected when the owner allows another party to drive the vehicle.

Red Flag Situation

Situation: An architect asks her secretary to take her personal car and deliver blueprints to a client across town. The secretary runs a red light and collides with a van. The van driver is seriously injured and sues the architect. The defendant's auto insurance did not include other-driver coverage. (This coverage is also referred to as an omnibus clause.)

Potential problem: The architect's insurer can deny coverage because the insured's policy did not cover other parties who may drive the insured's car.

Going Global

1. Insurance laws vary greatly throughout the world. In some countries, vehicle insurance is mandatory.

2. Many countries do not provide for no-fault insurance coverage.

3. Many domestic insurance policies do not cover a vehicle when the insured crosses the border into another country unless the insured obtains additional coverage.

Reducing Your Risks

1. Assess your vehicle insurance coverage on a regular basis to make sure the coverage is adequate.

2. If your company is engaged in transporting hazardous cargo, make certain the liability coverage is sufficient.

3. Review the deductible on your collision and compare the amount in premiums payments you will save by raising the deductible amount.

4. Make certain your company's policies cover all who may drive company vehicles.

5. Understand that the employer can be liable for any accidents caused by an employee within the scope of employment.

Sources of Information

1. More information on insurance is available at *http://www.swlearning.com/blaw/ fundamentals/fundamentals6e/fundamentals6e.html.* Go to "Interactive Study Guide" and click on Chapter 30, "Insurance, Wills, and Trusts."

2. To learn about vehicle insurance in your state, visit the Insurance Information Institute at *http://www.iii.org* and go to "Auto."

Void Title

(*See Sales*)

Voidable Title

(*See Sales*)

Ww

Warranty of Fitness for a Particular Purpose

(*See Implied Warranties*)

Warranty of Merchantability

(*See Implied Warranties*)

Workers' Compensation Insurance

(For additional information, *see Insurance.*)

Workers' compensation insurance provides coverage for employees who suffer a job-related injury or illness. State workers' compensation laws determine the categories of workers covered, the amount of and duration of compensation payments, and the administrative procedures for filing a claim.

Employees Covered: State laws provide a covered employee can receive compensation provided the injury suffered was within the course of employment and was the result of an accident. The worker is compensated even if the injury is due to his own

211

negligence. A worker who intentionally injures himself is not eligible for compensation.

Consequences of Receiving Workers' Compensation: In exchange for receiving workers' compensation, the employee generally relinquishes the right to file a lawsuit against the employer for negligence. If the injured worker determines the employer intentionally caused the injury, the worker can still file a lawsuit.

Red Flag Situation

Situation: While on a sales trip, an employee is injured in an auto accident and files for workers' compensation. The employer argues the worker is not covered because the accident occurred away from the company's premises.

Potential problem: As a general rule, employees not are covered by workers' compensation during the travel between home and workplace. An exception to this general rule is when the employee is a salesperson traveling on behalf of the employer.

Going Global

Employment laws vary greatly throughout the world. Many countries require employers to provide workers' compensation for workers injured within the scope of employment.

Reducing Your Risks

1. Remember that state workers' compensation laws are not the same in every state. If your company has employees in several states, make certain that you are properly contributing for all eligible workers in each state.

2. If your company chooses to be self-insured (rather than purchase workers' compensation insurance) be sure the company maintains its ability to pay claims, especially if the work is hazardous.

3. Understand that in certain circumstances a worker is covered during travel time.

Sources of Information

1. To learn more about workers' compensation, visit the National Labor Relations Board at *http://www.nlrb.gov*.

2. Additional information is available at *http://www.swlearning.com/blaw/fundamentals/fundamentals6e/fundamentals6e.html*. Go to "Interactive Study Guide" and click on Chapter 23, "Employment Law."

Wrongful Discharge

(For additional information, *see Contract, Employment Law* and *Tort.*)

Wrongful discharge occurs when an employee is fired and the firing violates a statute, contract, or a common law doctrine. A former employee may have a wrongful discharge claim even in an at-will employment situation.

Wrongful Discharge and Employment-At-Will: In an employment-at-will situation, no time period for the employment relationship is specified. The general idea is that the employee can quit at any time, and the employer can terminate the job at any time.

Recently the courts have held employers may be liable for wrongful discharge even in an employment-at-will situation. Courts have held discharges wrongful based on the following theories:

1. An implied contract may exist even in an employment-at-will situation. Assume a company provides all at-will employees with a policy manual stating no employee will be discharged without first being counseled as to inferior performance and given an opportunity to improve. The company fires an at-will employee following the first infraction and without counseling. The employee can claim breach of the implied contract contained in the policy manual.

2. The discharge is wrongful according to tort law. An at-will employee may still sue for wrongful discharge claiming intentional infliction of mental distress, fraud (in making certain promises), and defamation.

3. The discharge violates public policy. Assume an at-will employee is discharged for being a whistleblower, serving on a jury or cooperating with an agency investigating the employer. The employee may sue for wrongful discharge. (These discharges also violate certain state and federal statutes.)

Red Flag Situation

Situation: A health care organization is undergoing an investigation by a state regulatory agency. The organization discharges an at-will employee who has indicated a willingness to cooperate with investigators.

Potential problem: A court can find that the discharge was wrongful based on violation of public policy. (The discharge also violated statutes protecting those who cooperate in investigations.)

Going Global

1. An employee cannot be discharged in the United Kingdom without consulting with

the worker's trade union.

2. German law requires approval of the Works Council in order to discharge a worker.

3. In Mexico, a worker cannot be discharged except for reasons stated in the labor code.

Reducing Your Risks

1. Understand that an at-will employee may sue for wrongful discharge.

2. Review your company's personnel and policy manuals; provisions in these documents may create an implied contract with an at-will employee.

3. If you hire workers abroad, be familiar with labor laws in the host country prior to dismissing an employee.

Sources of Information

1. To learn more about foreign labor laws, go to *http://www.ilo.org*.

2. More information on wrongful discharge is available at
*http://www.swlearning.com/blaw/fundamentals/fundamentals6e/
fundamentals6e.html*. Go to "Interactive Study Guide" and click on Chapter 23, "Employment Law."

Wrongful Interference With a Contractual Relationship

(*See Torts*)

Wrongful Interference With An Economic Expectation

(*See Torts*)

Appendix A

The Constitution of the United States

We the People of the United States, in Order to form a more perfect Union, establish Justice, insure domestic Tranquility, provide for the common defence, promote the general Welfare, and secure the Blessings of Liberty to ourselves and our Posterity, do ordain and establish this Constitution for the United States of America.

ARTICLE I

Section 1. All legislative Powers herein granted shall be vested in a Congress of the United States, which shall consist of a Senate and House of Representatives.

Section 2. The House of Representatives shall be composed of Members chosen every second Year by the People of the several States, and the Electors in each State shall have the Qualifications requisite for Electors of the most numerous Branch of the State Legislature.

No Person shall be a Representative who shall not have attained to the Age of twenty five Years, and been seven Years a Citizen of the United States, and who shall not, when elected, be an Inhabitant of that State in which he shall be chosen.

Representatives and direct Taxes shall be apportioned among the several States which may be included within this Union, according to their respective Numbers, which shall be determined by adding to the whole Number of free Persons, including those bound to Service for a Term of Years, and excluding Indians not taxed, three fifths of all other Persons. The actual Enumeration shall be made within three Years after the first Meeting of the Congress of the United States, and within every subsequent Term of ten Years, in such Manner as they shall by Law direct. The Number of Representatives shall not exceed one for every thirty Thousand, but each State shall have at Least one Representative; and until such enumeration shall be made, the State of New Hampshire shall be entitled to chuse three, Massachusetts eight, Rhode Island and Providence Plantations one, Connecticut five, New York six, New Jersey four, Pennsylvania eight, Delaware one, Maryland six, Virginia ten, North Carolina five, South Carolina five, and Georgia three.

When vacancies happen in the Representation from any State, the Executive Authority thereof shall issue Writs of Election to fill such Vacancies.

The House of Representatives shall chuse their Speaker and other Officers; and shall have the sole Power of Impeachment.

Section 3. The Senate of the United States shall be composed of two Senators from each State, chosen by the Legislature thereof, for six Years; and each Senator shall have one Vote.

Immediately after they shall be assembled in Consequence of the first Election, they shall be divided as equally as may be into three Classes. The Seats of the Senators of the first Class shall be vacated at the Expiration of the second Year, of the second Class at the Expiration of the fourth Year, and of the third Class at the Expiration of the sixth Year, so that one third may be chosen every second Year; and if Vacancies happen by Resignation, or otherwise, during the Recess of the Legislature of any State, the Executive thereof may make temporary Appointments until the next Meeting of the Legislature, which shall then fill such Vacancies.

No Person shall be a Senator who shall not have attained to the Age of thirty Years, and been nine Years a Citizen of the United States, and who shall not, when elected, be an Inhabitant of that State for which he shall be chosen.

The Vice President of the United States shall be President of the Senate, but shall have no Vote, unless they be equally divided.

The Senate shall chuse their other Officers, and also a President pro tempore, in the Absence of the Vice President, or when he shall exercise the Office of President of the United States.

The Senate shall have the sole Power to try all Impeachments. When sitting for that Purpose, they shall be on Oath or Affirmation. When the President of the United States is tried, the Chief Justice shall preside: And no Person shall be convicted without the Concurrence of two thirds of the Members present.

Judgment in Cases of Impeachment shall not extend further than to removal from Office, and disqualification to hold and enjoy any Office of honor, Trust, or Profit under the United States: but the Party convicted shall nevertheless be liable and subject to Indictment, Trial, Judgment, and Punishment, according to Law.

Section 4. The Times, Places and Manner of holding Elections for Senators and Representatives, shall be prescribed in each State by the Legislature thereof; but the Congress may at any time by Law make or alter such Regulations, except as to the Places of chusing Senators.

The Congress shall assemble at least once in every Year, and such Meeting shall be on the first Monday in December, unless they shall by Law appoint a different Day.

Section 5. Each House shall be the Judge of the Elections, Returns, and Qualifications of its own Members, and a Majority of each shall constitute a Quorum to do Business; but a smaller Number may adjourn from day to day, and may be authorized to compel the Attendance of absent Members, in such Manner, and under such Penalties as each House may provide.

Each House may determine the Rules of its Proceedings, punish its Members for disorderly Behavior, and, with the Concurrence of two thirds, expel a Member.

Each House shall keep a Journal of its Proceedings, and from time to time publish the same, excepting such Parts as may in their Judgment require Secrecy; and the Yeas and Nays of the Members of either House on any question shall, at the Desire of one fifth of those Present, be entered on the Journal.

Neither House, during the Session of Congress, shall, without the Consent of the other, adjourn for more than three days, nor to any other Place than that in which the two Houses shall be sitting.

Section 6. The Senators and Representatives shall receive a Compensation for their Services, to be ascertained by Law, and paid out of the Treasury of the United States. They shall in all Cases, except

Treason, Felony and Breach of the Peace, be privileged from Arrest during their Attendance at the Session of their respective Houses, and in going to and returning from the same; and for any Speech or Debate in either House, they shall not be questioned in any other Place.

No Senator or Representative shall, during the Time for which he was elected, be appointed to any civil Office under the Authority of the United States, which shall have been created, or the Emoluments whereof shall have been increased during such time; and no Person holding any Office under the United States, shall be a Member of either House during his Continuance in Office.

Section 7. All Bills for raising Revenue shall originate in the House of Representatives; but the Senate may propose or concur with Amendments as on other Bills.

Every Bill which shall have passed the House of Representatives and the Senate, shall, before it become a Law, be presented to the President of the United States; If he approve he shall sign it, but if not he shall return it, with his Objections to the House in which it shall have originated, who shall enter the Objections at large on their Journal, and proceed to reconsider it. If after such Reconsideration two thirds of that House shall agree to pass the Bill, it shall be sent together with the Objections, to the other House, by which it shall likewise be reconsidered, and if approved by two thirds of that House, it shall become a Law.

But in all such Cases the Votes of both Houses shall be determined by Yeas and Nays, and the Names of the Persons voting for and against the Bill shall be entered on the Journal of each House respectively. If any Bill shall not be returned by the President within ten Days (Sundays excepted) after it shall have been presented to him, the Same shall be a Law, in like Manner as if he had signed it, unless the Congress by their Adjournment prevent its Return in which Case it shall not be a Law.

Every Order, Resolution, or Vote, to which the Concurrence of the Senate and House of Representatives may be necessary (except on a question of Adjournment) shall be presented to the President of the United States; and before the Same shall take Effect, shall be approved by him, or being disapproved by him, shall be repassed by two thirds of the Senate and House of Representatives, according to the Rules and Limitations prescribed in the Case of a Bill.

Section 8. The Congress shall have Power To lay and collect Taxes, Duties, Imposts and Excises, to pay the Debts and provide for the common Defence and general Welfare of the United States; but all Duties, Imposts and Excises shall be uniform throughout the United States;

To borrow Money on the credit of the United States;

To regulate Commerce with foreign Nations, and among the several States, and with the Indian Tribes;

To establish an uniform Rule of Naturalization, and uniform Laws on the subject of Bankruptcies throughout the United States;

To coin Money, regulate the Value thereof, and of foreign Coin, and fix the Standard of Weights and Measures;

To provide for the Punishment of counterfeiting the Securities and current Coin of the United States;

To establish Post Offices and post Roads;

To promote the Progress of Science and useful Arts, by securing for limited Times to Authors and Inventors the exclusive Right to their respective Writings and Discoveries;

To constitute Tribunals inferior to the supreme Court;

To define and punish Piracies and Felonies committed on the high Seas, and Offenses against the Law of Nations;

To declare War, grant Letters of Marque and Reprisal, and make Rules concerning Captures on Land and Water;

To raise and support Armies, but no Appropriation of Money to that Use shall be for a longer Term than two Years;

To provide and maintain a Navy;

To make Rules for the Government and Regulation of the land and naval Forces;

To provide for calling forth the Militia to execute the Laws of the Union, suppress Insurrections and repel Invasions;

To provide for organizing, arming, and disciplining, the Militia, and for governing such Part of them as may be employed in the Service of the United States, reserving to the States respectively, the Appointment of the Officers, and the Authority of training the Militia according to the discipline prescribed by Congress;

To exercise exclusive Legislation in all Cases whatsoever, over such District (not exceeding ten Miles square) as may, by Cession of particular States, and the Acceptance of Congress, become the Seat of the Government of the United States, and to exercise like Authority over all Places purchased by the Consent of the Legislature of the State in which the Same shall be, for the Erection of Forts, Magazines, Arsenals, dock-Yards, and other needful Buildings;-And

To make all Laws which shall be necessary and proper for carrying into Execution the foregoing Powers, and all other Powers vested by this Constitution in the Government of the United States, or in any Department or Officer thereof.

Section 9. The Migration or Importation of such Persons as any of the States now existing shall think proper to admit, shall not be prohibited by the Congress prior to the Year one thousand eight hundred and eight, but a Tax or duty may be imposed on such Importation, not exceeding ten dollars for each Person.

The privilege of the Writ of Habeas Corpus shall not be suspended, unless when in Cases of Rebellion or Invasion the public Safety may require it.

No Bill of Attainder or ex post facto Law shall be passed.

No Capitation, or other direct, Tax shall be laid, unless in Proportion to the Census or Enumeration herein before directed to be taken.

No Tax or Duty shall be laid on Articles exported from any State.

No Preference shall be given by any Regulation of Commerce or Revenue to the Ports of one State over those of another: nor shall Vessels bound to, or from, one State be obliged to enter, clear, or pay Duties in another.

No Money shall be drawn from the Treasury, but in Consequence of Appropriations made by Law; and a regular Statement and Account of the Receipts and Expenditures of all public Money shall be published from time to time.

No Title of Nobility shall be granted by the United States: And no Person holding any Office of Profit or Trust under them, shall, without the Consent of the Congress, accept of any present, Emolument, Office, or Title, of any kind whatever, from any King, Prince, or foreign State.

Section 10. No State shall enter into any Treaty, Alliance, or Confederation; grant Letters of Marque and Reprisal; coin Money; emit Bills of Credit; make any Thing but gold and silver Coin a Tender in Payment of Debts; pass any Bill of Attainder, ex post facto Law, or Law impairing the Obligation of Contracts, or grant any Title of Nobility.

No State shall, without the Consent of the Congress, lay any Imposts or Duties on Imports or Exports, except what may be absolutely necessary for executing its inspection Laws: and the net Produce of all Duties and Imposts, laid by any State on Imports or Exports, shall be for the Use of the Treasury of the United States; and all such Laws shall be subject to the Revision and Controul of the Congress.

No State shall, without the Consent of Congress, lay any Duty of Tonnage, keep Troops, or Ships of War in time of Peace, enter into any Agreement or Compact with another State, or with a foreign Power, or engage in War, unless actually invaded, or in such imminent Danger as will not admit of delay.

ARTICLE II

Section 1. The executive Power shall be vested in a President of the United States of America. He shall hold his Office during the Term of four Years, and, together with the Vice President, chosen for the same Term, be elected, as follows:

Each State shall appoint, in such Manner as the Legislature thereof may direct, a Number of Electors, equal to the whole Number of Senators and Representatives to which the State may be entitled in the Congress; but no Senator or Representative, or Person holding an Office of Trust or Profit under the United States, shall be appointed an Elector.

The Electors shall meet in their respective States, and vote by Ballot for two Persons, of whom one at least shall not be an Inhabitant of the same State with themselves. And they shall make a List of all the Persons voted for, and of the Number of Votes for each; which List they shall sign and certify, and transmit sealed to the Seat of the Government of the United States, directed to the President of the Senate. The President of the Senate shall, in the Presence of the Senate and House of Representatives, open all the Certificates, and the Votes shall then be counted. The Person having the greatest Number of Votes shall be the President, if such Number be a Majority of the whole Number of Electors appointed; and if there be more than one who have such Majority, and have an equal Number of Votes, then the House of Representatives shall immediately chuse by Ballot one of them for President; and if no Person have a Majority, then from the five highest on the List the said House shall in like Manner chuse the President. But in chusing the President, the Votes shall be taken by States, the Representation from each State having one Vote; A quorum for this Purpose shall consist of a Member or Members from two thirds of the States, and a Majority of all the States shall be necessary to a Choice. In every Case, after the Choice of the President, the Person having the greater Number of Votes of the Electors shall be the Vice President. But if there should remain two or more who have equal Votes, the Senate shall chuse from them by Ballot the Vice President.

The Congress may determine the Time of chusing the Electors, and the Day on which they shall give their Votes; which Day shall be the same throughout the United States.

No person except a natural born Citizen, or a Citizen of the United States, at the time of the Adoption of this Constitution, shall be eligible to the Office of President; neither shall any Person be eligible to that Office who shall not have attained to the Age of thirty five Years, and been fourteen Years a Resident within the United States.

In Case of the Removal of the President from Office, or of his Death, Resignation or Inability to discharge the Powers and Duties of the said Office, the same shall devolve on the Vice President, and the Congress may by Law provide for the Case of Removal, Death, Resignation or Inability, both of the President and Vice President, declaring what Officer shall then act as President, and such Officer shall act accordingly, until the Disability be removed, or a President shall be elected.

The President shall, at stated Times, receive for his Services, a Compensation, which shall neither be increased nor diminished during the Period for which he shall have been elected, and he shall not receive within that Period any other Emolument from the United States, or any of them.

Before he enter on the Execution of his Office, he shall take the following Oath or Affirmation: "I do solemnly swear (or affirm) that I will faithfully execute the Office of President of the United States, and will to the best of my Ability, preserve, protect and defend the Constitution of the United States."

Section 2. The President shall be Commander in Chief of the Army and Navy of the United States, and of the Militia of the several States, when called into the actual Service of the United States; he may require the Opinion, in writing, of the principal Officer in each of the executive Departments, upon any Subject relating to the Duties of their respective Offices, and he shall have Power to grant Reprieves and Pardons for Offenses against the United States, except in Cases of Impeachment.

He shall have Power, by and with the Advice and Consent of the Senate to make Treaties, provided two thirds of the Senators present concur; and he shall nominate, and by and with the Advice and Consent of the Senate, shall appoint Ambassadors, other public Ministers and Consuls, Judges of the supreme Court, and all other Officers of the United States, whose Appointments are not herein otherwise provided for, and which shall be established by Law; but the Congress may by Law vest the Appointment of such inferior Officers, as they think proper, in the President alone, in the Courts of Law, or in the Heads of Departments.

The President shall have Power to fill up all Vacancies that may happen during the Recess of the Senate, by granting Commissions which shall expire at the End of their next Session.

Section 3. He shall from time to time give to the Congress Information of the State of the Union, and recommend to their Consideration such Measures as he shall judge necessary and expedient; he may, on extraordinary Occasions, convene both Houses, or either of them, and in Case of Disagreement between them, with Respect to the Time of Adjournment, he may adjourn them to such Time as he shall think proper; he shall receive Ambassadors and other public Ministers; he shall take Care that the Laws be faithfully executed, and shall Commission all the Officers of the United States.

Section 4. The President, Vice President and all civil Officers of the United States, shall be removed from Office on Impeachment for, and Conviction of, Treason, Bribery, or other high Crimes and Misdemeanors.

Article III

Section 1. The judicial Power of the United States, shall be vested in one supreme Court, and in such inferior Courts as the Congress may from time to time ordain and establish. The Judges, both of the supreme and inferior Courts, shall hold their Offices during good Behaviour, and shall, at stated Times, receive for their Services a Compensation, which shall not be diminished during their Continuance in Office.

Section 2. The judicial Power shall extend to all Cases, in Law and Equity, arising under this Constitution, the Laws of the United States, and Treaties made, or which shall be made, under their Authority;-to all Cases affecting Ambassadors, other public Ministers and Consuls;-to all Cases of admiralty and maritime Jurisdiction;-to Controversies to which the United States shall be a Party;-to Controversies between two or more States;-between a State and Citizens of another State;-between Citizens of different States;-between Citizens of the same State claiming Lands under Grants of different States, and between a State, or the Citizens thereof, and foreign States, Citizens or Subjects.

In all Cases affecting Ambassadors, other public Ministers and Consuls, and those in which a State shall be a Party, the supreme Court shall have original Jurisdiction. In all the other Cases before mentioned, the supreme Court shall have appellate Jurisdiction, both as to Law and Fact, with such Exceptions, and under such Regulations as the Congress shall make.

The Trial of all Crimes, except in Cases of Impeachment, shall be by Jury; and such Trial shall be held in the State where the said Crimes shall have been committed; but when not committed within any State, the Trial shall be at such Place or Places as the Congress may by Law have directed.

Section 3. Treason against the United States, shall consist only in levying War against them, or, in adhering to their Enemies, giving them Aid and Comfort. No Person shall be convicted of Treason unless on the Testimony of two Witnesses to the same overt Act, or on Confession in open Court.

The Congress shall have Power to declare the Punishment of Treason, but no Attainder of Treason shall work Corruption of Blood, or Forfeiture except during the Life of the Person attainted.

Article IV

Section 1. Full Faith and Credit shall be given in each State to the public Acts, Records, and judicial Proceedings of every other State. And the Congress may by general Laws prescribe the Manner in which such Acts, Records and Proceedings shall be proved, and the Effect thereof.

Section 2. The Citizens of each State shall be entitled to all Privileges and Immunities of Citizens in the several States.

A Person charged in any State with Treason, Felony, or other Crime, who shall flee from Justice, and be found in another State, shall on Demand of the executive Authority of the State from which he fled, be delivered up, to be removed to the State having Jurisdiction of the Crime.

No Person held to Service or Labour in one State, under the Laws thereof, escaping into another, shall, in Consequence of any Law or Regulation therein, be discharged from such Service or Labour, but shall be delivered up on Claim of the Party to whom such Service or Labour may be due.

Section 3. New States may be admitted by the Congress into this Union; but no new State shall be formed or erected within the Jurisdiction of any other State; nor any State be formed by the Junction of two or more States, or Parts of States, without the Consent of the Legislatures of the States concerned as well as of the Congress.

The Congress shall have Power to dispose of and make all needful Rules and Regulations respecting the Territory or other Property belonging to the United States; and nothing in this Constitution shall be so construed as to Prejudice any Claims of the United States, or of any particular State.

Section 4. The United States shall guarantee to every State in this Union a Republican Form of Government, and shall protect each of them against Invasion; and on Application of the Legislature, or of the Executive (when the Legislature cannot be convened) against domestic Violence.

ARTICLE V

The Congress, whenever two thirds of both Houses shall deem it necessary, shall propose Amendments to this Constitution, or, on the Application of the Legislatures of two thirds of the several States, shall call a Convention for proposing Amendments, which, in either Case, shall be valid to

all Intents and Purposes, as part of this Constitution, when ratified by the Legislatures of three fourths of the several States, or by Conventions in three fourths thereof, as the one or the other Mode of Ratification may be proposed by the Congress; Provided that no Amendment which may be made prior to the Year One thousand eight hundred and eight shall in any Manner affect the first and fourth Clauses in the Ninth Section of the first Article; and that no State, without its Consent, shall be deprived of its equal Suffrage in the Senate.

ARTICLE VI

All Debts contracted and Engagements entered into, before the Adoption of this Constitution shall be as valid against the United States under this Constitution, as under the Confederation.

This Constitution, and the Laws of the United States which shall be made in Pursuance thereof; and all Treaties made, or which shall be made, under the Authority of the United States, shall be the supreme Law of the Land; and the Judges in every State shall be bound thereby, any Thing in the Constitution or Laws of any State to the Contrary notwithstanding.

The Senators and Representatives before mentioned, and the Members of the several State Legislatures, and all executive and judicial Officers, both of the United States and of the several States, shall be bound by Oath or Affirmation, to support this Constitution; but no religious Test shall ever be required as a Qualification to any Office or public Trust under the United States.

ARTICLE VII

The Ratification of the Conventions of nine States shall be sufficient for the Establishment of this Constitution between the States so ratifying the Same.

AMENDMENT I [1791]

Congress shall make no law respecting an establishment of religion, or prohibiting the free exercise thereof; or abridging the freedom of speech, or of the press; or the right of the people peaceably to assembly, and to petition the Government for a redress of grievances.

Amendment II [1791]

A well regulated Militia, being necessary to the security of a free State, the right of the people to keep and bear Arms, shall not be infringed.

Amendment III [1791]

No Soldier shall, in time of peace be quartered in any house, without the consent of the Owner, nor in time of war, but in a manner to be prescribed by law.

Amendment IV [1791]

The right of the people to be secure in their persons, houses, papers, and effects, against unreasonable searches and seizures, shall not be violated, and no Warrants shall issue, but upon probable cause, supported by Oath or affirmation, and particularly describing the place to be searched, and the persons or things to be seized.

Amendment V [1791]

No person shall be held to answer for a capital, or otherwise infamous crime, unless on a presentment or indictment of a Grand Jury, except in cases arising in the land or naval forces, or in the Militia, when in actual service in time of War or public danger; nor shall any person be subject for the same offence to be twice put in jeopardy of life or limb; nor shall be compelled in any criminal case to be a witness against himself, nor be deprived of life, liberty, or property, without due process of law; nor shall private property be taken for public use, without just compensation.

Amendment VI [1791]

In all criminal prosecutions, the accused shall enjoy the right to a speedy and public trial, by an impartial jury of the State and district wherein the crime shall have been committed, which district shall have been previously ascertained by law, and to be informed of the nature and cause of the accusation; to be confronted with the witnesses against him; to have compulsory process for obtaining witnesses in his favor, and to have the Assistance of Counsel for his defence.

Amendment VII [1791]

In Suits at common law, where the value in controversy shall exceed twenty dollars, the right of trial by jury shall be preserved, and no fact tried by jury, shall be otherwise re-examined in any Court of the United States, than according to the rules of the common law.

Amendment VIII [1791]

Excessive bail shall not be required, nor excessive fines imposed, nor cruel and unusual punishments inflicted.

Amendment IX [1791]

The enumeration in the Constitution, of certain rights, shall not be construed to deny or disparage others retained by the people.

Amendment X [1791]

The powers not delegated to the United States by the Constitution, nor prohibited by it to the States, are reserved to the States respectively, or to the people.

Amendment XI [1798]

The Judicial power of the United States shall not be construed to extend to any suit in law or equity, commenced or prosecuted against one of the United States by Citizens of another State, or by Citizens or Subjects of any Foreign State.

Amendment XII [1804]

The Electors shall meet in their respective states, and vote by ballot for President and Vice-President, one of whom, at least, shall not be an inhabitant of the same state with themselves; they shall name in their ballots the person voted for as President, and in distinct ballots the person voted for as Vice-President, and they shall make distinct lists of all persons voted for as President, and of all persons voted for as Vice-President, and of the number of votes for each, which lists they shall sign and certify, and transmit sealed to the seat of the government of the United States, directed to the President of the Senate;-The President of the Senate shall, in the presence of the Senate and House of Representatives, open all the certificates and the votes shall then be counted;-The person having the greatest number of votes for President, shall be the President, if such number be a majority of the whole number of Electors appointed; and if no person have such majority, then from the persons having the highest numbers not exceeding three on the list of those voted for as President, the House of Representatives shall choose immediately, by ballot, the President. But in choosing the President, the votes shall be taken by states, the representation from each state having one vote; a quorum for this purpose shall consist of a member or members from two-thirds of the states, and a majority of all states shall be necessary to a choice. And if the House of Representatives shall not choose a President whenever the right of choice shall devolve upon them, before the fourth day of March next following, then the Vice-President shall act as President, as in the case of the death or other constitutional disability of the President.-The person having the greatest number of votes as Vice-President, shall be the Vice-President, if such number be a majority of the whole number of Electors appointed, and if no person have a majority, then from the two highest numbers on the list, the Senate shall choose the Vice-President; a quorum for the purpose shall consist of two-thirds of the whole number of Senators, and a majority of the whole number shall be necessary to a choice. But no person constitutionally ineligible to the office of President shall be eligible to that of Vice-President of the United States.

Amendment XIII [1865]

Section 1. Neither slavery nor involuntary servitude, except as a punishment for crime whereof the party shall have been duly convicted, shall exist within the United States, or any place subject to their jurisdiction.

Section 2. Congress shall have power to enforce this article by appropriate legislation.

Amendment XIV [1868]

Section 1. All persons born or naturalized in the United States, and subject to the jurisdiction thereof, are citizens of the United States and of the State wherein they reside. No State shall make or enforce any law which shall abridge the privileges or immunities of citizens of the United States; nor shall any State deprive any person of life, liberty, or property, without due process of law; nor deny to any person within its jurisdiction the equal protection of the laws.

Section 2. Representatives shall be apportioned among the several States according to their respective numbers, counting the whole number of persons in each State, excluding Indians not taxed. But when the right to vote at any election for the choice of electors for President and Vice President of the United States, Representatives in Congress, the Executive and Judicial officers of a State, or the members of the Legislature thereof, is denied to any of the male inhabitants of such State, being twenty-one years of age, and citizens of the United States, or in any way abridged, except for participation in rebellion, or other crime, the basis of representation therein shall be reduced in the proportion which the number of such male citizens shall bear to the whole number of male citizens twenty-one years of age in such State.

Section 3. No person shall be a Senator or Representative in Congress, or elector of President and Vice President, or hold any office, civil or military, under the United States, or under any State, who having previously taken an oath, as a member of Congress, or as an officer of the United States, or as a member of any State legislature, or as an executive or judicial officer of any State, to support the Constitution of the United States, shall have engaged in insurrection or rebellion against the same, or given aid or comfort to the enemies thereof. But Congress may by a vote of two-thirds of each House, remove such disability.

Section 4. The validity of the public debt of the United States, authorized by law, including debts incurred for payment of pensions and bounties for services in suppressing insurrection or rebellion, shall not be questioned. But neither the United States nor any State shall assume or pay any debt or obligation incurred in aid of insurrection or rebellion against the United States, or any claim for the loss or emancipation of any slave; but all such debts, obligations and claims shall be held illegal and void.

Section 5. The Congress shall have power to enforce, by appropriate legislation, the provisions of this article.

AMENDMENT XV [1870]

Section 1. The right of citizens of the United States to vote shall not be denied or abridged by the United States or by any State on account of race, color, or previous condition of servitude.

Section 2. The Congress shall have power to enforce this article by appropriate legislation.

AMENDMENT XVI [1913]

The Congress shall have power to lay and collect taxes on incomes, from whatever source derived, without apportionment among the several States, and without regard to any census or enumeration.

AMENDMENT XVII [1913]

Section 1. The Senate of the United States shall be composed of two Senators from each State, elected by the people thereof, for six years; and each Senator shall have one vote. The electors in each State shall have the qualifications requisite for electors of the most numerous branch of the State legislatures.

Section 2. When vacancies happen in the representation of any State in the Senate, the executive authority of such State shall issue writs of election to fill such vacancies: Provided, That the legislature of any State may empower the executive thereof to make temporary appointments until the people fill the vacancies by election as the legislature may direct.

Section 3. This amendment shall not be so construed as to affect the election or term of any Senator chosen before it becomes valid as part of the Constitution.

AMENDMENT XVIII [1919]

Section 1. After one year from the ratification of this article the manufacture, sale, or transportation of intoxicating liquors within, the importation thereof into, or the exportation thereof from the United States and all territory subject to the jurisdiction thereof for beverage purposes is hereby prohibited.

Section 2. The Congress and the several States shall have concurrent power to enforce this article by appropriate legislation.

Section 3. This article shall be inoperative unless it shall have been ratified as an amendment to the Constitution by the legislatures of the several States, as provided in the Constitution, within seven years from the date of the submission hereof to the States by the Congress.

AMENDMENT XIX [1920]

Section 1. The right of citizens of the United States to vote shall not be denied or abridged by the United States or by any State on account of sex.

Section 2. Congress shall have power to enforce this article by appropriate legislation.

AMENDMENT XX [1933]

Section 1. The terms of the President and Vice President shall end at noon on the 20th day of January, and the terms of Senators and Representatives at noon on the 3d day of January, of the years in which such terms would have ended if this article had not been ratified; and the terms of their successors shall then begin.

Section 2. The Congress shall assemble at least once in every year, and such meeting shall begin at noon on the 3d day of January, unless they shall by law appoint a different day.

Section 3. If, at the time fixed for the beginning of the term of the President, the President elect shall have died, the Vice President elect shall become President. If the President shall not have been chosen before the time fixed for the beginning of his term, or if the President elect shall have failed to qualify, then the Vice President elect shall act as President until a President shall have qualified; and the Congress may by law provide for the case wherein neither a President elect nor a Vice President elect shall have qualified, declaring who shall then act as President, or the manner in which one who is to act shall be selected, and such person shall act accordingly until a President or Vice President shall have qualified.

Section 4. The Congress may by law provide for the case of the death of any of the persons from whom the House of Representatives may choose a President whenever the right of choice shall have devolved upon them, and for the case of the death of any of the persons from whom the Senate may choose a Vice President whenever the right of choice shall have devolved upon them.

Section 5. Sections 1 and 2 shall take effect on the 15th day of October following the ratification of this article.

Section 6. This article shall be inoperative unless it shall have been ratified as an amendment to the Constitution by the legislatures of three-fourths of the several States within seven years from the date of its submission.

AMENDMENT XXI [1933]

Section 1. The eighteenth article of amendment to the Constitution of the United States is hereby repealed.

Section 2. The transportation or importation into any State, Territory, or possession of the United States for delivery or use therein of intoxicating liquors, in violation of the laws thereof, is hereby prohibited.

Section 3. This article shall be inoperative unless it shall have been ratified as an amendment to the Constitution by conventions in the several States, as provided in the Constitution, within seven years from the date of the submission hereof to the States by the Congress.

AMENDMENT XXII [1951]

Section 1. No person shall be elected to the office of the President more than twice, and no person who has held the office of President, or acted as President, for more than two years of a term to which some other person was elected President shall be elected to the office of President more than once. But this Article shall not apply to any person

holding the office of President when this Article was proposed by the Congress, and shall not prevent any person who may be holding the office of President, or acting as President, during the term within which this Article becomes operative from holding the office of President or acting as President during the remainder of such term.

Section 2. This article shall be inoperative unless it shall have been ratified as an amendment to the Constitution by the legislatures of three-fourths of the several States within seven years from the date of its submission to the States by the Congress.

AMENDMENT XXIII [1961]

Section 1. The District constituting the seat of Government of the United States shall appoint in such manner as the Congress may direct:

A number of electors of President and Vice President equal to the whole number of Senators and Representatives in Congress to which the District would be entitled if it were a State, but in no event more than the least populous state; they shall be in addition to those appointed by the states, but they shall be considered, for the purposes of the election of President and Vice President, to be electors appointed by a state; and they shall meet in the District and perform such duties as provided by the twelfth article of amendment.

Section 2. The Congress shall have power to enforce this article by appropriate legislation.

AMENDMENT XXIV [1964]

Section 1. The right of citizens of the United States to vote in any primary or other election for President or Vice President, for electors for President or Vice President, or for Senator or Representative in Congress, shall not be denied or abridged by the United States, or any State by reason of failure to pay any poll tax or other tax.

Section 2. The Congress shall have power to enforce this article by appropriate legislation.

AMENDMENT XXV [1967]

Section 1. In case of the removal of the President from office or of his death or resignation, the Vice President shall become President.

Section 2. Whenever there is a vacancy in the office of the Vice President, the President shall nominate a Vice President who shall take office upon confirmation by a majority vote of both Houses of Congress.

Section 3. Whenever the President transmits to the President pro tempore of the Senate and the Speaker of the House of Representatives his written declaration that he is unable to discharge the powers and duties of his office, and until he transmits to them a written declaration to the contrary, such powers and duties shall be discharged by the Vice President as Acting President.

Section 4. Whenever the Vice President and a majority of either the principal officers of the executive departments or of such other body as Congress may by law provide, transmit to the President pro tempore of the Senate and the Speaker of the House of Representatives their written declaration that the President is unable to discharge the powers and duties of his office, the Vice President shall immediately assume the powers and duties of the office as Acting President.

Thereafter, when the President transmits to the President pro tempore of the Senate and the Speaker of the House of Representatives his written declaration that no inability exists, he shall resume the powers and duties of his office unless the Vice President and a majority of either the principal officers of the executive department or of such other body as Congress may by law provide, transmit within four days to the President pro tempore of the Senate and the Speaker of the House of Representatives their written declaration that the President is unable to discharge the powers and duties of his office. Thereupon Congress shall decide the issue, assembling within forty-eight hours for that purpose if not in session. If the Congress, within twenty-one days after receipt of the latter written declaration, or, if Congress is not in session, within twenty-one days after Congress is required to assemble, determines by two-thirds vote of both Houses that the President is unable to discharge the powers and duties of his office, the Vice President shall continue to discharge the same as Acting President; otherwise, the President shall resume the powers and duties of his office.

AMENDMENT XXVI [1971]

Section 1. The right of citizens of the United States, who are eighteen years of age or older, to vote shall not be denied or abridged by the United States or by any State on account of age.

Section 2. The Congress shall have power to enforce this article by appropriate legislation.

AMENDMENT XXVII [1992]

No law, varying the compensation for the services of the Senators and Representatives, shall take effect, until an election of Representatives shall have intervened.

Index

About TEXERE

Texere, a progressive and authoritative voice in business publishing, brings to the global business community the expertise and insights of leading thinkers. Our books educate, enlighten, and entertain, and provide an intersection where our authors and our readers share cutting edge ideas, practices, and innovative solutions. Texere seeks to cultivate, enhance, and disseminate information that illuminates the global business landscape.

www.thomson.com/learning/texere

About the typeface

This book was set in 10 point Adobe Garamond Condensed. Adobe Garamond was created in the sixteenth century by Claude Garamond, a French printer and publisher. This typeface is known for its versatile and elegant design, which has made it a standard among book designers and printers for four centuries.